Making
the World
Safe for
Democracy

Making
the World
Safe for
Democracy

*A Century of Wilsonianism
and Its Totalitarian Challengers*

BY AMOS PERLMUTTER

The University of North Carolina Press

Chapel Hill & London

Designed by Richard Hendel
Set in Carter & Cone Galliard
by Eric M. Brooks
Illustration © 1997 Ed Lindlof
Manufactured in the United States of America

The paper in this book meets the guidelines for
permanence and durability of the Committee on
Production Guidelines for Book Longevity of the
Council on Library Resources.

Library of Congress Cataloging-in-Publication Data
Perlmutter, Amos.
Making the world safe for democracy: a century
of Wilsonianism and its totalitarian challengers /
by Amos Perlmutter.
p.   cm.
Includes bibliographical references and index.
ISBN 0-8078-2365-1 (alk. paper)
1. World politics—20th century—Case studies.
2. Wilson, Woodrow, 1856–1924—Influence.   I. Title.
D445.P395   1998
973.91'3—dc21   97-9883
                CIP

01   00   99   98   97   5   4   3   2   1

This book is dedicated
with love and affection to
Sharon Elizabeth Watts,
a wonderful human being.

CONTENTS

This book describes, analyzes, and evaluates the three most significant world orders of the twentieth century: the Wilsonian order, the Leninist/Stalinist order, and the Hitlerian order. The major reason for this choice is that world order can be set only by a hegemonial power, an industrial, technological, and military power. The three world systems were anchored in three hegemonial states: the United States, the Soviet Union, and Nazi Germany.

I further claim that the ambitions and orientations of these three great powers were ideological. The ideology represented the motivations, purposes, directions, and consequences of the three pretenders to world order. Only these three states could organize and mobilize an industrial, military, and political system to enable them not only to establish a world order but also to influence the international system. All hegemonial powers, by definition of being military, industrial, and economic powers, are interventionist. The Wilsonian influence and role in interventionism set the pattern for most American interventions. These interventions were covert through the use of agents and other diplomatic, political, and military means. U.S. intervention in Mexico in 1913, America's "secret war against Bolshevism," and its subsequent intervention in the Russian civil war (1917–20) demonstrate the methods and steps of the American style of intervention: the withdrawal of American diplomatic representatives, the imposition of an arms embargo on the regime, the blockade of the ports, the use of the marines, and the imposition of moral and economic sanctions. The use of very limited military intervention, as in the case of Mexico and the Russian civil war, and of intelligence gathering and covert action was enhanced by Woodrow Wilson beginning in 1914. The conspicuous use of covert action during Wilson's time, which would return with vengeance under Harry S. Truman, Dwight D. Eisenhower, and John F. Kennedy, demonstrates that in the age of nationalism and national sovereignty, nineteenth-century forms of imperialism would not be supported by public opinion and Congress. Therefore, regimes had to be subverted by covert action. To respond to liberal critics and advisers, who suggested that the United States should refrain from military intervention in Russia, Wilson argued for the respectability of the principle of nonintervention, and yet hypocritically he did the opposite. He was highly involved in clandestine action, witnessed by Mexico and the Russian civil war.[1] The Wilson administration's operations employed techniques later used in the Cold War against international communism. According to David Fogelsong, "Among the most significant legacies of the Wilson years were the formative experiences that inclined such men as Allen and John Foster Dulles to rely on propaganda and covert action when they led the Central Intelligence Agency and the State Department in the 1950s."[2] Since Wilson, every American president has avoided being candid with Congress and the American people, thereby undermining the support he sought for his foreign policy. "Wilson's unwillingness to be frank with Congress and the American people also undermined support for his highest priority, the League of Nations."[3] "In the wake of the Cold War and the collapse of the Soviet system Woodrow Wilson continues to be a central figure—perhaps the central figure—in American thinking about international relations. For many, Wilson represents an inspiring liberal internationalism committed to the principles of self-determination and nonintervention. Others invoke Wilson as an exemplar of humanitarian intervention around the world or as a paragon of the carefully defined and restricted use of force."[4]

We certainly distinguish the American system from the Nazi and Soviet ones. The United States, from Woodrow Wilson to Bill Clinton, has espoused a stable, peaceful, and free-market-oriented system. The United States, hegemonial by definition of its superior economic and military power, which clearly demonstrated itself in World War II and the Cold War, had no imperial ambitions. To identify the United States as an imperial power, as many intellectual revisionist historians have done, is faulty. America wielded influence by virtue of its modern innovative ideas, skills in technology, marketing, and creation of a consumer society rather than by its domination of other peoples. The definition of an empire must include the motivation, desire, and practices of ruling others. Except for a few islands in the Pacific and the Caribbean which the United States acquired for strategic purposes, especially to prevent Japanese domination, the American people and the American political system rejected imperialism in the classical sense. Of course, the westward movement (Louisiana Purchase, wars with Mexico and Canada) represented an American Manifest Destiny, but its goal was to establish a democratic system from coast to coast. The United States had the opportunity to conquer and occupy Mexico, Cuba, and islands in the Caribbean, but doing so was always rejected and unacceptable to the American people and the American politicians.

Imperialism, however, was fundamental to communist and Nazi political systems. One cannot explain communism without expansion. Their orientations and aspirations required the establishment of a classless world order dominated by Moscow (the Leninist/Stalinist idea) and the formation of a racially dominated Europe (the Nazi idea). Neither communism nor Nazism could have survived without a combination of imperialist and ideological dedication.

One could inquire whether fascism aimed to create an international order. Undoubtedly, fascism is an imperialist and cultural ideology. It is aggressive, championing war and the *cadaverprinzip* (principle of death). It calls for a youthful, radical nationalist revolution in politics, art, and literature. In short, dying young but heroically is as totalitarian as Nazism and communism. The reason why I do not deal with the fascist international order is that the only ruling fascist regime was that of Benito Mussolini in Italy, which was not a major or hegemonial power.[5] Italy's industrial and military capabilities were insufficient to establish a world order. Italy's inability to occupy the Balkans without the aid of Nazi Germany in World War II clearly demonstrated the limitations of its industrial military power.[6] Fascism certainly had all the ideological ingredients for a totalitarian world order, but it was not anchored in a major industrial state and military power.

Fascism certainly was an influential ideology, which meshed well with radical nationalism. The fascist movement was more universal than Nazism. Fascist parties and movements did emerge in Central East Europe, the Balkans, the Arab Middle East, and Latin America. But the major distinction between it and Nazism was that Nazism was a racial movement and fascism was not. Therefore, fascism has greater appeal to people the Nazis would consider "inferior." After all, there were Jewish fascists in Italy. The political science departments of universities in Mussolini's Italy were dominated by fascists, several of them Jews. And the Lehi-Stern Gang, a Jewish terrorist group in Palestine, flirted with fascist ideas. In this sense, fascism could have become a more influential international movement than Nazism, which was restricted to the Germanic Aryan races. But having no center of political power, no central hegemonial state, it failed to establish the kind of international order that Hitler briefly established and that Lenin and Stalin established for most of the twentieth century.

This book is inspired to some extent by neorealist theories, but not completely. It also is a contribution to this school in the sense that ideology has strengthened the security and sustenance of the hegemonial states.[7] Ideology cements the raison d'être of modern hegemonial powers. The Soviet Union without ideology would still have been a major power. Its ideology fortified and expanded the country's security and influence. The Wilsonian and American international order sought a stable, peaceful international system to enhance American democracy and free trade. For if the world, especially Europe, were influenced by the Wilsonian principles, American security would be enhanced and strengthened. American exceptionalism is an instrument of American interventionism and expansion.

This book also aims to demonstrate not only that the aspiration for world order is an important element of hegemonial powers' security orientations but also that ideology—considered by the neorealist school as a domestic element that does not, on the whole, influence the international system, so that it really does not matter whether a regime is committed to one ideology or another—is nevertheless a most significant element in the structure of a nation's security.

Once again, this demonstrates that only hegemonial powers are inclined to establish a world order. It is, however, not imperative, as has been the case of the United States after 1989. Both Nazism and communism have been defeated; fascism had no home, no foundation to establish such an order, and Wilsonianism has been restricted by American economic and domestic burdens. But it is in the nature of international relations that under certain circumstances, intervention will not suffice, and ideology must inspire hegemonial aspirations to a world order. World order is not necessarily a prescription for enhanced security, even if it is perceived to be so. But as the only hegemonial power left, the United States did not preoccupy itself with the largesse of expansive Wilsonianism. After 1989, like Alice in Wonderland, the cat left and the smile remained; so is the case of Wilsonianism. The United States still acts haphazardly, speaking and proclaiming a neo-Wilsonian world order. But it is not now willing to pay the price that it was willing to pay during the Cold War. Up until 1941, the United States did not find a world order in the national interest. Between 1941 and 1989, the period of World War II and the Cold War, the United States reversed its isolationism to become an interventionist power willing to pay the highest price to sustain a world order that would contain the Soviet Union militarily and psychologically. To understand this behavior, one has to examine the relationship between hegemony, ideology, and power, the major themes of this book. Even if the rivalry was between nuclear superpowers, it was enveloped in fierce ideological commitments.

The hegemonial rivalry between the United States and the USSR was, according to some authors[8] (with whom I agree), also linked to mission. Mission became the ingredient of political and power position. In other words, the rivalry could not be expressed merely in power terms. It had to be explained by ideological, utopian, and other mission-oriented rhetorics. If hypothetically China becomes, in the twenty-first century, a hegemonial power rivaling the United States, it is quite plausible that ideology will grease the rivalry so that the American people can see it in black-and-white terms, the only way it was possible to mobilize the American people in World War II and the Cold War. Mobilization must be both exclusive and inclusive; domestic and foreign support are the foundations for sustaining the system. Thus an emergent hegemon rivaling the United States may re-invent an American version of a new world order, one that is morally and economically superior to its rival. It is true that hegemonial powers tend to create a balance of power, which is another euphemism for stability and order. Yet ideological spooks may tear asunder the power of a hegemon that can no longer rely merely on power, economic, industrial, and military.

ACKNOWLEDGMENTS

No book can be written without the wisdom of others, and I refer to the vast literature that deals with various aspects of the theme from which the idea of the book emerged. This literature can be found in the bibliography and references. The Wilsonian scholar Arthur Link of Princeton University, who indefatigably labored in Wilson's papers and is their official editor, laid the foundations for all of us in his monumental five-volume work. My understanding of Woodrow Wilson, in addition to excellent recent biographies and monographs, comes from my good friend and one of the readers and critics of this book, Professor Robert Tucker of the School of Advanced International Studies at Johns Hopkins University in Washington, D.C., a leading scholar in the field of American and international foreign policy, who has written a seminal work on Thomas Jefferson. I wish I could have at my disposal his forthcoming book on President Wilson. My old friend Professor Kenneth W. Waltz of the University of California-Berkeley, the leading theorist on what is now known as neorealism in international relations, extensively reviewed my work. Although I have not accepted some of his views concerning the Cold War, both he and Bob Tucker have helped me to see the connection between ideology, power, and hegemonialism that is the major theme of my book. I have learned considerably from my friend Professor Michael Burleigh of the London School of Economics, who has pioneered in the field of the Third Reich and clearly pointed out that its foreign policy was based on racial theories and that Nazism should be distinguished from fascism and should not be considered a species of fascism, as some authors would prefer. I, therefore, have not accepted the proposition that Nazism is a species of fascism. Hitler and the Nazis were the first modern theorists who based their foreign and imperial politics on a racial theory. My understanding of Stalin and Stalinism comes from the writings of my good friends and esteemed scholars Professor Richard Pipes at Harvard and Professor Robert Conquest of the Hoover

Institution at Stanford, who, ahead of all Western scholars, explained in detail the Soviet system as a "Grand Terror regime." Pipes and Conquest, long before other Western scholars, demonstrated the Stalin that people such as Alexander Solzhenitsyn and others would finally persuade us of. Richard Pipes identified Lenin as a forerunner of Stalinism and the Soviet Union as an imperial hegemonial power. My late friend and former editor of *Survey*, Leopold Labedz, whose knowledge of international communism was unrivaled, taught me more about communism than any other writer or scholar. I would like to acknowledge the following people who helped to shape this book. First, I thank my good friend Joyce Selzer of Harvard University Press and my former dedicated assistant Laura Natelson and current assistant David Levin. Timothy Dickenson, a savant and original thinker, has helped me to sharpen some of my concepts and saved me from errors. But the real person behind the publication of this book is the editor's editor, Lewis Bateman, who ran the manuscript efficiently and alerted me to some criticisms that I would have otherwise failed to appreciate. Last but not least, I am grateful to my friend Sharon Elizabeth Watts, without whom this manuscript would remain in disorder. I dedicate the book to her. It would be an exercise in futility, as some authors insist, to claim that all faults are mine. Who else?

Making
the World
Safe for
Democracy

The Age of Totalitarianism
New and Old International Orders

After the Soviet system collapsed in 1989, American president George Bush called for the establishment of a "new world order," which would replace the old bipolar nuclear balance of terror, a placid state of cold war. The collapse of this order created alarm and fear that the absence of a predictable world order might threaten international stability, security, and peace. The search for a "new" world order was all the rage in the press and within the halls of academia, all trying to make sense of a world that no longer appeared to have a defining "order." The Persian Gulf War was seen as a stepping-stone in that direction, but although there was widespread optimism, it was uncalled for because the president and others misperceived the meaning of a "new world order." A new world order would be one that is mission-oriented, ideologically motivated, and politically revolutionary. What took place after 1989, in contrast, was a counterrevolution.

The fall of the last totalitarian movement (i.e., communism) did not bring about a need, motivation, or ideological purpose for establishing any world order, new or otherwise. The issues facing the international system today have nothing to do with ideology. The return of neocommunist power under the guise of social democracy, which followed the fall of the Soviet Empire, is certainly not a triumph of democracy and free trade, even if Soviet totalitarianism is dead. Once again, this does not mean that the United States does not cease to be a hegemonial industrial, military, economic, and technological power or that the role required of such a power does not exist. The case of the Gulf War of 1991 demonstrates the power of a single hegemon and that it—and only it—can guarantee the balance of power, international order, and stability. The emergence of new nationalisms, ethnicity, and nuclear dwarfs has not led to the trauma that some authors expected of a post–Cold War world. In fact, India and Pakistan have not destroyed each other; they are small nuclear powers. Israel has sustained stability in the Middle East by claiming to have a "bomb in the basement" even if the proof of Israel's nuclear capability is still in the shadows. Speculations surrounding Israel's nuclear power are the desired goal of the makers of Israeli foreign policy, from David Ben-Gurion to the most recent prime minister, in hopes of deterring the Arabs, who would like to annihilate Israel, from doing so. These speculations played a tremendous role of deterrence, certainly in the case of the Gulf War, when Saddam Hussein—itching to launch missiles with chemical warheads—did not do so because of the knowledge and understanding of the price he, his regime, his people, and his state would pay. In fact, not unlike the balance of terror which was established between the two superpowers, the absence of what is called "bipolarity" does not mean the international order is in chaos or that there is any more threat stemming from pygmies and pariahs than from giants and leviathans.

The argument that the post-1989 world is a return to the pre-1919 era is false, primarily because of the hegemonial and nuclear power of the United States, the decisive role it plays in the stability of Europe, the organization of the North Atlantic Treaty Organization (NATO) as a military, political, and ideological system, and the absence of a loose, military industrial power—Nazi or Soviet—in the international arena. So if Yugoslavia is reminiscent of the situation I describe in Chapter 2, there is no chance that another Hitler will emerge to destabilize either the European or the international order. Nuclear weapons will modify such aspirations, as they modified Stalinist expansionism.

The post-1989 international system is characterized by disorder, national and ethnic competition, the threat of fundamental-ism to Arab regimes, and nuclear proliferation among small nations.[1] This conflict certainly threatens the Arab world but is hardly a threat to the international system. For instance, Islamic fundamentalism will not create a new world order; neither Iran nor Sudan, the sources of this movement, is a real threat to hegemonial powers, who are in a position to annihilate them if necessary. And except for Islamic fundamentalism there is no revolutionary or progressive (or pseudo-progressive) ideological movement in the post-1989 era. As we will see in the following chapters, in this century ideological movements could exert in-fluence *only* when they emerged from hegemonial powers, such as the United States, the Soviet Union, and Nazi Germany.

Hegemony without ideology represents the ability or the in-clination to intervene to protect the balance of power. Those who fail to realize that the American mission and its Wilsonian-ism have been extinguished are in for a rude awakening. Wilsoni-anism is on a low burner today. The emergence of a rival power will rekindle it and arrest any Hitlerian or Stalinist avarice.

In this book, I examine the development of three world or-ders—Nazism, communism, and democratic liberalism—and contrast them with the absence of world orders today. The inter-pretive frame of reference which I offer responds to cataclysmic developments that took place in this century at the end of World War I, which resulted in the end of monarchical, military, bu-reaucratic elite domination of major states in Europe, the col-lapse of three empires (Austro-Hungarian, Ottoman, and Rus-sian), the rise of mass movements and of charismatic political figures (such as Lenin, Hitler, and Mussolini), and the rise of mil-itant radical revolutionary nationalism combined with romanti-cism and the militarization of politics. It is in this context that three world orders emerged.

In contrast, following the collapse of communism, none of the above circumstances exist. Mass ideological movements are a matter of the past. A cynical world is not prey for ideological moorings and aspirations. The information revolution has de-stroyed the totalitarian propaganda machinery. The globalization of communication and national relationships has destroyed the stereotypes that played a key role, especially in fascism and Nazism. Further, none of the conditions that prevailed in 1919 are applicable today. The world is safer for democracy than it ever was, despite ethnic struggles in Bosnia, Chechnia, Somalia, Iraq, or other peripheries. Certainly issues concerning the adjustment of former colonies of the Soviet Empire are important, but they are not ideological. They are ethnic and nationalistic. They do not threaten the international system as did Nazism, fascism, and communism. The issues and concerns in play in 1919 are light-years away from the world after 1989. For those who cite Russia's possible return to a communist system that could lead to a new world order, I would point out that if Russia does return to some form of neocommunism, as some of the Eastern European states have experimented with, it will not be a messianic communism with a totalitarian party state, propaganda, and police apparatus and institutions. The election of Boris Yeltsin forced the choice between going back to communism or choosing moderate re-form and crude democracy; the Russian electorate voted with their feet.

In the absence of such developments in the international system, there is very little chance that a movement similar to those post-1919 will rise to settle issues which, after all, are nonexistent today. The question is not whether there is a chance that a new world order will arise. The search for such an order is an exercise in intellectual and political futility. In the absence of revolutionary movements and aggressive superpowers, a new world order could emerge again only if a rival hegemonial power emerges.

The twentieth century has been called many things, including the age of totalitarianism, the age of ideology, and the age of the Gulags and gas chambers, but it also was the age of emergent liberalism, democracy, and freedom. The three most prominent ideological and international orders were democracy, Nazism, and communism; although they emerged separately and independently, they nevertheless soon came into direct confrontation with one another. Confrontations between these ideological and political movements dominated Europe, America, and the colonial world during the twentieth century. In this book, I relate how these three world orders emerged after 1919, why they failed, and what were the consequences for the international system.

This book is also a study of the philosophy and conceptual framework of America's foreign policy in the twentieth century, a century dominated by attempts to establish a new world order. It is also a study of the challenges to this new world order, in the guise of communism and Nazism. It has relevance today because of America's seemingly never-ending search for a new international order to replace that of the Cold War.

OLD AND NEW WORLD ORDERS

The founding father of the search for a new world order, President Woodrow Wilson, set forth the essential goals and principles of American foreign policy for decades to come. His new world order was intended to be liberal, internationalist, antirevolutionary, capitalist, pacific in nature, and exceptionalist. Ingredients of his worldview may be seen throughout the twentieth century, from Wilson to Bill Clinton, although sometimes in modified form. The vision of America as an exceptional nation with democratic, economic, and liberal institutions embodied the best possible body politic obtainable. This vision was New Freedom dressed up in the authority of ideals transcending national boundaries and ideologies. It led to a moral foreign policy which involved the view that American democratic ideals were transportable merely because they were socially desirable; this policy was often accompanied by the use of force to crush revolutionary nationalism and communism even if employed in a moral and noble cause.

The most serious challengers to the implementation of Wilson's new order were two rival and ruthless world orders: Lenin and Stalin's classless world order and Hitler's Nazi racist world order. The struggle between Wilsonianism and these two competing orders would define American foreign policy in the twentieth century. The Bolshevik world order sought to destroy capitalist liberalism and its institutions; communism in its early days held some universal appeal until it became obvious that it had jettisoned its egalitarian dreams. Hitler had no universalist dreams as did Bolshevism; his thinking was restricted to the triumph of the German Aryan race over "inferior" races. Hitler's world order was restrictive, destructive, and vindictive.

Wilson's great gift as a leader was his ability to mobilize American moral, idealistic, and institutional instruments and ideas toward the purpose of creating an American-inspired world order on liberal-capitalist lines. Wilson had conceived this vision as a result of the hegemonial emergence of the United States as a world power at the turn of the twentieth century. The difference between the Wilsonian and the Leninist and Hitlerian orders was that the American order was not achieved by force or violence—American values and goods were marketed to the world through persuasion. Americans could be mobilized to struggle against the evils of fascism and communism. Paradoxically, the Wilsonian ideal is still ongoing today despite *a lack of universal doctrine or ideology against which to wage peace*. There is no longer an overarching threat which challenges the American idea. With the end of the Cold War and the demise of Bolshevism—at least as an all-encompassing world threat—the raison d'être to contain revolutionary and totalitarian regimes no longer exists. Present-day Wilsonianism continues to be used as the basis for American foreign policy, *but it has lost its power to mobilize*. The American people cannot be mobilized to embrace a struggle against nebulous foes, complicated civil wars, or even Islamic fundamentalism in the way that they were mobilized to combat Nazism and communism.

The strength of Wilsonianism is that despite American impotence and confusion in the face of ethnic, nationalist, and inter-ethnic wars such as in Bosnia, it nevertheless intervened. None of these struggles are characterized by a worldview or by overarching and threatening ideologies looking to engulf or enslave. The Cold War Western NATO coalition has not proven very useful in this new and confusing climate, as its hesitant way of dealing with the crises in Bosnia and Yugoslavia has indicated. But this is not a permanent condition. With NATO seemingly appearing ineffectual, the craving for stability becomes even stronger. The climate seems chaotic, with ethnic strife in various parts of the former Soviet Union and East Central Europe, with uncertainty surrounding the future of Russia—where "Democrats" try to fend off a spirit of irrational nationalism—and with neomercantilist postcommunism in the Eastern European states of Poland and Hungary. Certainly the ripped fragments of Brezhnevite and Titoist chains have done nothing but excite old animosities and hatreds, while the acquisition of nuclear weapons and technology by smaller and irresponsible nations like Iran, Iraq, and North Korea do not threaten a nuclear war, as some theorists mistakenly predicted during the Cold War. I take serious issue with the argument that nuclear rogues threaten the international system. Countries with nuclear weapons have not attempted to blackmail because the United States as a single hegemon is dedicated, as were the two Cold War superpowers, to preserving the peace. Nuclear weapons may have been the major factor in preserving the peace. And there is no reason why they will not continue to do so.

This book examines the ideological premises of three world orders, the connection between power and ideology, and the men and leaders who created and attempted to institutionalize them—Woodrow Wilson's, Lenin's, and Hitler's world orders—as well as the issue of whether the United States should try to define a new world order in the twenty-first century.

Implicit in the attempt to create a new world order is the idea that a world is an ideological construct, a set of directions based on political experience and theories of the various founders of twentieth-century world orders. The idea is that an aspiration for world order, or an ideology of how international order dictates the behavior of nations, is better than, say, spheres of influence, a balance of power, or the discredited League of Nations and its successor, the impotent United Nations. The question is whether international security would be better guaranteed by a more modest, less romantic, nonideological, pragmatic system of spheres of influence as the governing system of international order and security. Can the experience of the twentieth century be a guide for the twenty-first century international system? Was the twentieth century uniquely ideological? We certainly cannot predict the course of events into the next century—say hypothetically if China or Germany become nuclear superpowers. Strategically, therefore, if the rivalry for domination of the international system involves three nuclear powers, will we then see a different architecture? Is it possible that powers 1 and 2 would combine against power 3? This certainly could have happened in the prenuclear age. It does not matter how many nuclear weapons one possesses; a few are enough to destroy states, societies, and the environment. Even if one single power is damaged, the other will be utterly so as well. Therefore, ideology may no longer sustain a tripartite nuclear hegemonial rivalry. Mission orientation will not suffice to deter an ambitious hegemonial power. Nuclear weapons will. These, of course, are important and highly speculative questions. Some of these propositions may not be unreasonable; they could be probable. If so, the relationship between hegemony, ideology, and power would be reduced to a simple relationship between hegemony and nuclear power. It could substitute, at least in the international system, for a deterrent or a threat. For a democracy like the United States, naked power alone—even if it represents a national interest—will not suffice to mobilize domestic forces and resources and rekindle a real power without which no arsenal can be effective. Thus it is—despite neorealist theories—true that some form of ideology willy-nilly will for the unforeseen future play a most significant role in projecting or failing to project American power. Not that totalitarian states have not been successful in using ideology (Nazi Germany and the Soviet Union certainly did so), but they mobilized human and material resources through the use of brutal police power. This, of course, was not especially true of the Soviet Union in World War II, for it had to defend its territory at all costs, and Father Joseph Stalin and Mother Russia combined to create an ideological shield. So mobilization in totalitarian states does not demand consent. Fear will suffice. Thus a threat of a totalitarian state possessing nuclear weapons is related to its ideological commitments, without which it cannot exercise total power and total mobilization. Patriotism not Marxism served and saved the Stalinist regime. It was very close to collapse a few weeks after the Nazi invasion. Stalin's power was restored by patriotism and brute force. Ideology went down the drain. Stalingrad was not defended in the name of Leninism. But once Stalin was victorious, he resurrected ideology as an instrument of Soviet imperialism and expansionism. The canard of a cooperative Stalin will not wash.

Basic questions that speak to international world orders include:

(1) How was a new world order conceived by its protagonists, Wilson, Hitler, and Lenin?

(2) Why and how did they fail?

(3) What shadow did their legacies cast over the rest of this century?

(4) Whose ideology finally prevailed, as we near the end of this century?

(5) What sort of an international system can we expect in the twenty-first century?

A new world order is an international political system that can emerge only when an older system has been transformed and has exhausted itself. This usually occurs after a great war or when a revolutionary party emerges in the international system, such as the Nazi and Communist Parties. By international order, I mean a state of relations among nations governed by some overarching order or empire, a universal state of relations, be it bipolarity, multipolarity, or just plain anarchy, which may be described as disorderly order.

The modern world order that has existed since the French Revolution has been a mixed one combining empires and nation-states in an international system; this order is generally unpredictable. A new world order, in contrast, is mission oriented, seeking stability in the name of a hegemonial ideology that is intended to dominate the world system; such were the orders of Wilsonianism, Nazism, and communism. Between 1805 and 1815, European centricity was governed by a Napoleonic imperial hegemonial order. From the 1815 Congress of Vienna to the

1848 nationalist revolutions, the European order was dominated by a coalition of Russia, Austria, and dynastic Prussia, with no dominant hegemon. The period between 1848 and 1914 saw an almost ideal European balance of power, a delicate balance marked by imperialist and colonial drive. World War I would end the classical European-centered balance of power. The twentieth century then came to be dominated by three contending approaches to international order, three aspiring hegemonial powers, one championed by American president Woodrow Wilson, one by Vladimir Lenin, and one by Adolf Hitler. World War I put an end to the classical European balance of power, to be sure, but it also left in its wake a Hobbesian international order in Central and Eastern Europe. Lesser successor regimes were hammered out of the paradoxical mold of self-determination, an ill-fitting combination of the ideas of Wilson and Lenin. These successor regimes were volatile and fragile patchworks, paper-thin authorities and institutions, all of which tended to contribute to a growing European and international climate of disorder.

Order of a sort was restored by Stalin and Hitler, wolf brothers under the skin who were remarkably alike in their dedication to destroy the international order and replace it with their own versions marked by naked aggression, expansion, and a merciless and ruthless ideology. Order was brought about through war, occupation, destruction, and plunder, not to mention the Gulag and the purges in the Soviet Union, as well as the destruction of the Slavic peoples and the extermination of the Jews in Europe under the Nazis. These world orders were aggressive and expansionist. Lenin, Stalin, and Hitler all sought to achieve their utopias—Lenin and Stalin's a classless world order dominated by the Soviet Union, Hitler's a racist world dominated by Nazi Germany—through force. It was a very expensive and amoral way to achieve order. But superior force, overweening ambition, and the most destructive war in history destroyed Hitler's world order. Lenin's world order and that of his heirs collapsed on its own, prompted by perpetual purges, militarism, economic inefficiency, and the big lie.

Hitler's order was destroyed by the Nazi-Soviet war of 1941–45 and the final drive of the Anglo-American alliance in 1944–45. The crushing defeat of Nazism did not create a balance of power or end totalitarianism, but rather resulted in a new international order anchored in the lone remaining superpowers. This was an international system based on balance of nuclear power, a super-power hegemonial rivalry inhibited by the balance of terror known as the Cold War.

The world of Lenin, Stalin, and Hitler was discredited from its inception, and the communist model survived by sheer domestic police and brute force. When the ideology was exhausted, the lie could pose as the truth only because it was propped up by the political police and secret institutions such as the NKVD and the KGB. Once the police structures were destroyed, the state itself began to crumble. These two world orders, once exposed, were vulnerable to collapse. The struggle between the United States and the USSR was conducted in the name of ideology but was actually a hegemonial conflict. The atomic bomb permanently altered the nature of the post-1945 world. For a brief time (1945–50), the United States enjoyed nuclear hegemony, which ended when the Soviets developed a nuclear weapon. This marked the onset of bipolarity, a new world order in which two hegemonial camps created a balance of terror. The struggle between the two was carried into the Third World as well because bipolarity and atomic exclusivity left the United States and the USSR to arrange the structure of the international order.

With the end of nuclear deterrence and bipolarity, the world did not revert to the one of 1919 with the attendant dangers of ethnic rivalries and nationalist aspirations. The result has been to destabilize Soviet-Asiatic republics and similar dangers in the Ukraine and Russia, as well as the implosion of Yugoslavia and the formal splintering of Czechoslovakia.

Under the bipolar system a nuclear war was avoided for four decades. In the wake of the collapse of the Soviet and Eastern European communist states, the world seemed to return to an even more intensely Hobbesian state reminiscent of the dangerous years between the two world wars. Since 1989, except for the

United States and Western Europe (i.e., Germany and the rest of Europe), new states have emerged from the collapse of the Soviet Union, with the potential for even more in Russia. The two states created by the Versailles Treaty of 1919, Czechoslovakia and Yugoslavia, collapsed. The latter plunged into an ethnic, cleansing civil war. But it did not upset the balance of power in Europe.

With Clinton's second term (1997) in power in the United States, still struggling to formulate a consistent foreign policy, it is important to examine international security issues now, to see what structural arrangements will replace bipolarity and how they will affect U.S. security. The problems associated with the presence of only one hegemon—the United States—are compounded by the spread of nuclear, chemical, and biological means of warfare.

At the end of the twentieth century the world is once again confronted by an aggressive and disorderly atmosphere such as that which led to the rise of these totalitarian ideologies—represented now in the rise of ethnicity and nationalism. The events of 1989 and the subsequent instability clearly demonstrate that the absence of an imperial hegemonial power leaves these conflicting states and ethnic groups at the mercy of the international system. The hesitant and anti-imperial United States, the world's lone superpower, faces a world arena in which the lack of willpower to establish a new world order is patently obvious. It is clear that only empires or great powers with the inclination and will can lead to the creation of an international order.

It is my contention that the only way for a new world order to arise in the twenty-first century is if the United States becomes involved in a confrontation with another hegemonial power. It could be China or Germany but it must be an industrial-military power. But there is no world state equivalent to Hitler's Nazi Germany or Lenin and Stalin's Soviet Union. The raison d'être for a world order, old or new, does not exist today. Any effort to revive it is an exercise in futility. American presidents have learned since Vietnam that an American policy, however well meant, cannot bear fruit without the consent of the American people and Congress. The American polity is not designed to have an efficient foreign policy. Wilson failed to persuade both the people and Congress, and his new world order died embryonically. The American post–World War II Cold War policy begun by Harry Truman and continued by his successors until the end of the Bush administration still proclaims its mission and ideology. In the current world environment, neither Islamic fundamentalism nor petty intertribal or interethnic battles such as those in Bosnia and Chechnia present the all-encompassing threats posed by international communism and racist pan-German Nazi ideology. There is no new hegemon to challenge the United States. With prospects of nuclear power in the hands of politically reckless leaders of radical Moslem regimes, as well as an impotent, absurd, and sorely strained United Nations, prospects do not bode well for an immediate reappearance of a new world order.

This book is based mainly on secondary sources and published documents. It is an effort at interpretation and analysis. The intellectual apparatus used here does not depend on the discovery of earth-shaking newly uncovered documents but is more in the realm of political theory than diplomatic history. It is an effort at intellectual understanding of the twentieth-century international system. It is not another textbook of international relations, with the requisite chapters on realism, neorealism, and idealism. It is an effort to conceive a conceptual framework for the understanding of an era dominated by totalitarianism, ideology, and mission and the interrelationship between hegemony, ideology, and power. The comparative analysis between Wilson's, Hitler's, and Lenin's and Stalin's orders produces a different approach to the study of international relations and especially brings an end to the anachronistic concept of a new world order where there is none. No world order can be defended or organized by solitary hegemonial power. The United States today is unwilling to use its military force for any purpose except the defense of national interest, not for a great utopian NATO dream. The current U.S. involvement in Bosnia does not fit any theory of international relations and certainly does not represent American national interest. Whatever the consequences for America's intervention here, no new doctrine or mission will be established on its foundations. In fact, the Holbrooke doctrine of Bosnian intervention demonstrates the futility and the lack of realism which is artificially infused to revive a dead mentalité. American intervention in Bosnia represented by the Dayton Agreements is a strategic creep in the Balkans. Thus post-1989 American interventions are on the cheap: the cases of Somalia and Bosnia. But that did not prevent the demonstration of American might in the Gulf War, which was still on the cheap. In fact, the design of American military power after Vietnam has been based on technology and gadgetry under the doctrine that not one soldier can be lost or captured. This does not deny the existence of a neo-Wilsonian passion, which I said earlier is not predictable but can reemerge. The United States demonstrated during the Cold War what the red lines were, from Berlin to Korea and back to Berlin. Yet the unencumbered and free American intervention in Bosnia after long oscillation, that is, the Dayton Agreements, demonstrates that the sleeping giant is a giant nevertheless. America's ability to intervene relates very much to its military and nuclear domination, which has been unrivaled since 1945–50. What does it mean? Do we have any doubts that the United States would not dare intervene in a disintegrating Yugoslavia and that the Soviets would have to face their own quagmire, as they did in Afghanistan? So bipolarity is not always a panacea for the balance of power, even if it was crucial in the maintenance of the international system after 1945. The real reason, once again, was the nuclear preponderance of the rivals and the nuclear balance of terror. This sustained the stable order which continues today. The absence of ideology and a rival hegemon did not bring an end to forms of neo-Wilsonianism, however crude.

What order we will find in the twenty-first century is far from predictable. But it will be closer to nineteenth-century balance of power and concerts of the powers than to the ideology that infused and sustained the twentieth-century hegemonial powers' missions and utopias. I hope that this study will persuade the doubters that the Wilsonian imperative is not dead but remains on a low burner. Naturally, the United States will continue to champion human rights, political representation, competitive political parties, free press, and free markets, but not in the context of utopian zealousness. The United States will continuously face the dilemma between supporting international human rights and American business.

President Clinton's national security adviser Anthony Lake has proclaimed that he is a neo-Wilsonian. The president's intervention in Bosnia, however reluctant, demonstrates that America's hegemonial position is unchallenged. For more than three years the Europeans demonstrated their impotence in bringing an end to the war in Bosnia. To fulfill a Wilsonian utopia, the support of the American people and Congress is needed, but above all the unrestricted use of America's military and economic power is required. The foundation for Clinton's Bosnia policy, in contrast, is modified Wilsonianism, which is more in tune with the Weinberger-Perry doctrine of noninvolvement in a war until it has the support of the American people. We proclaimed our exit from Bosnia before we entered it. All American actions in Bosnia are governed by the fear of angering Congress and the American people, lest American boys come back home in bags. The very fact that the U.S.-NATO force is unwilling to pursue the International Court of Justice's efforts to hunt Bosnian war criminals demonstrates that the Wilson-Carter human rights policy is subservient to the policy of pragmatism—constantly looking over one's shoulder to assess the attitudes of Congress and the public. This cannot promise either a new world order or the resurrection of Wilsonianism, an ideology that was defeated before it began.

CHAPTER I

Radicalization, Mobilization, and the Post-1919 International Chaos

The three world orders that dominated the twentieth century—democracy, communism, and fascism—emerged between 1919 and 1939 in a chaotic international environment. This environment included the devastating effects of World War I (the most destructive war to interrupt the long history of nineteenth-century peace); the growth of state power, accompanied and challenged by radical nationalism, ethnicity, and ideology; the emergence of organized and disciplined single-party totalitarian movements; the radicalization of the working classes; and the rise of mass movements. These occurrences were aided by the destruction of the Ottoman, Russian, and Austro-Hungarian empires; the Balkanization and fragmentation of much of Central and Eastern Europe; the decline of constitutionalism and democracy; and the emergence of chaotic social and economic conditions in the immediate aftermath of the war, which produced serious social crises that led to extreme solutions.[1]

The most remarkable aspect of the international developments between 1919 and 1939 was the complete abdication of responsibility by the Great Powers. Britain, for example, became enmeshed in neoisolationism, concentrating on the empire and dominions, defining itself as an Atlantic rather than a European power. France, the largest continental power with the largest army, so feared a *resurrected* Germany that it became the vindictive enforcer of the punitive and territorial measures of the Versailles Treaty. Instead of coming to terms with Germany, the French concocted alliances with all the small powers (e.g., the Little Entente with Romania, Czechoslovakia, and Yugoslavia), which were exercises in futility because none of these powers contributed to France's security.

The ease with which Germany and later Russia would gain control over East-Central European territories was not only a result of the failure of the Great Powers to intervene but of the internecine and fratricidal national and ethnic struggles within the East-Central European and Balkan cocoon. As Joseph Rothschild states:

> Given this constellation of predatory, indifferent, and ineffective Great Powers, a constellation that it could neither prevent nor even control, East Central Europe might nevertheless have achieved at least minimal power-credibility if it had been able to achieve internal regional solidarity and some system of mutual assistance. But this alternative, too, was negated by the multiple divisions and rivalries that were born of competing territorial claims, ethnic-minority tensions, socioeconomic poverty, mutually irritating national psychologies, and sheer political myopia. These factors transformed the area's internal relations into a cockpit and facilitated Hitler's program of conquest. It is scarcely an exaggeration to suggest that as a general rule in interwar East Central Europe, common borders entailed hostile relations. Thus, the "blame" for the demise of the region's independence must be charged to its own fundamental weaknesses, the instability of its institutions, and its irresponsible governments, as well as to the active and passive faults of the Great Powers.[2]

It was obvious that "the main component of the several revisionist-irredentist territorial disputes in interwar East Central Europe was the ethnic one."[3] The various ethnic, nationality, and religious divisions searched for some definition of nationhood. According to Rothschild, "Standing politically midway between state-nations and ethnic minorities were those peoples who were officially defined as belonging to the former but felt themselves not only culturally distinct from, but also politically and economically exploited by, the dominant part of that same state-nation."[4] Economically, "East Central Europe was less productive, less literate, and less healthy than West Central and Western Europe."[5]

There were rich agricultural areas, but the political system inhibited any serious economic development, whether free capitalism or state intervention in the economy. Neither one was clearly established or successful. East European dictatorships that emerged between 1919 and 1939 were not mass-mobilized modernist dictatorships like the all-inclusive totalitarian systems of communism and Nazism which would develop in the Soviet Union and Germany. They either "failed or refused to elicit mass support."[6] Nevertheless, the radical rightist movements were inspired by fascist and Nazi ideologies, even in the absence of successful totalitarian mass-mobilization parties. The radical right parties, from which many authoritarian dictators and intellectuals emerged, were *völkisch*, and they fought against the "Judaization" of culture. Jews were blamed for instilling radical socialist, if not communist, ideologies at the expense of the peasant folk. The strength of radical right parties was proportional to the number of Jewish minorities in the area, itself an index of contact with the commercial world, and unquestionably the radical right was the foundation from which the pro-Nazi collaborators would later emerge. Not that such political parties and groups did not exist elsewhere, such as in France or pre-Hitlerian Germany, but they were fringe forces whose impact at best, in the case of France, was among the intellectuals (for example, Action Française).[7] There is no question that a convergence took place as soon as the Nazi movement became popular and successful in the late 1920s. Certainly Hitler's coming to power in 1933 overwhelmed and overshadowed the right-wing radicals, who now sought support from Nazi Germany and looked upon Hitler as the savior of Europe. Curiously enough, Hitler represented to them the quintessence of Europeanism, and these parties and groups supported Hitler's occupation forces after 1940 with great enthusiasm and hope. These parties on the whole governed the allied states of unoccupied Europe such as Hungary and Croatia during World War II. The Petain-Laval Vichy regime (1942–44), although in occupied territory, also fits into this category. During World War II, the Ustasi in Croatia, the Iron Guard in Romania, and the Arrow Cross in Hungary, all neo-Nazi, neofascist movements, were clients of Hitler, who did not have to occupy these territories for they made serious contributions to the Waffen SS and to German war efforts.

From the point of view of international politics and diplomacy, the most serious development obviously was the rise of the Leninist-Stalinist USSR and Nazi Germany. The two most significant totalitarian movements of modern times would emerge in the Soviet Union and Germany.[8] The arena for exercising their aggressions and territorial aspirations was Central and Eastern Europe, and for good reasons. Hungary, Czechoslovakia, Poland, Serbia (Yugoslavia), Romania, Bulgaria, Albania, and Greece were all run by authoritarian regimes (with the exception of Czechoslovakia), coalitions of radical nationalists, racists, and anti-Semites. As Rothschild wrote, "Indeed, it appears that the only really potent internationalistic ideology in the area at that time was neither Marxism, on the left hand, nor dynastic loyalism, on the right, but anti-Semitism based on both conviction and expedience. This, in turn, provided an ideological bond and precondition for eventual collaboration with the Nazis, including the administration of wartime genocide."[9]

Not only were they authoritarian but they also were economically unstable. Their boundaries and territories were mostly artificial, created by the Versailles Treaty, ignoring the existence of ethnic and national groups. Table 1 tells us much about the results of the Paris Peace Treaties of Versailles, St. Germain, Trianon, Neuilly, and Lausanne. This table clearly demonstrates a total lack of stability of governments challenged by minorities who had never lived together in a single nation-state.

Instead of a world safe for democracy, as wrongly prophesied by U.S. president Woodrow Wilson, the world became safe for autocracy and the emergence of the most radical, authoritarian,

TABLE I.
Extremism and Authoritarianism in
Central-Eastern Europe, 1921–1938

State	Minorities (approx. population, 1914)	Type of Regime/ Radical Political Parties
Austria	22% Czechs and Slovaks, 17% Poles, 12% Ruthenians, 7.5% Southern Slavs, 3% Italians, 1% Romanians	Fascist, 1933–36
Hungary	15% Romanians, 10% Germans, 9% Croats, 9% Slovaks, 6% Serbs, 3% Ruthenians	Peak of fascist/ Nazi strength, 1937–38
Czechoslovakia	24% Germans, 16% Slovaks, 8% Magyars, 3.8% Ruthenians	Democratic, but with local fascist movement: Gayda, Slovak Hlinka Party
Romania	9% Magyars, 7% Jews, 4% Germans, 2% Bulgarians, 5% Russians and Ukrainians, 4% Others	Authoritarian monarchy, rise of Nazi-like Iron Guard
Poland	16% Ukrainians, 11% Jews, 5% Russians, 4% Germans	(1) Nationalist dictatorship of Pilsudsky, 1926 (2) Nationalist authoritarian colonels, 1936–39
Serbia (Yugoslavia)	22% Croats, 9% Slovenes, 4% Germans, 4% Magyars, 4% Albanians	Authoritarian monarchy, rise of Croatian Nazi Ustasi, from 1929
Albania	13% Serbs, Greeks, and Turks	Dictatorship of Ahmad Zog, Albanian Nationalist Front

Source: John A. Lukacs, *The Great Powers and Eastern Europe*
(New York: American Book Company, 1953), 32–34.

racist, anti-Semitic, fascist, and Nazi-like protest movements of minorities within the Polish, Czech, Yugoslav, and Hungarian states. The territorial loss for some countries was as serious as the gain of territory was for others. Austria lost territory to Czechoslovakia, Poland, Italy, Romania, and Yugoslavia. Hungary lost territory to Romania, Czechoslovakia, Austria, Yugoslavia, Italy, and Poland. The only ones who gained territory were Czechoslovakia and Poland. And this is not to mention Germany's loss of territory to France, Belgium, Denmark, Poland, Lithuania, and Czechoslovakia, which of course would become a source of irredenta that would help the rise of Hitler and Nazism. Germans bitterly resented that the Versailles Treaty had incorporated the Sudentenland into Czechoslovakia and considered Czechs and the Slovaks inferior races; they bitterly resented being dominated by those they considered foreigners.[10] Not only were these many unstable states and territories challenged by their own domestic minorities and fascist radical nationalist movements (and later Nazi parties), they also violated each others' territory by efforts to adjust their own lost territories. This was the case with Poland and its unsuccessful effort to incorporate Russian-Ukrainian territory, as well as the Czech occupation of Teschen Polish territory.

Central and Eastern European countries were not the only ones where fascist, communist, and radical nationalist and authoritarian parties emerged. They also appeared in Finland, Lithuania, Latvia, Estonia, Greece, and Bulgaria. Thus most of Central Europe from the Baltic to the Black Sea was replete with extremism and authoritarianism between 1921 and 1939. Militarism, coups d'état, radicalism, and racial strife characterized much of the era between 1919 and 1939 in Central and Eastern Europe. And the emergence of the USSR and Nazi Germany would complete the total demise of Versailles and of the grand Wilsonian dreams.

Between Germany and Russia, there developed a most serious vacuum of illusory independent states, which would become the target of both aggressive communism and Nazism. As long as Eastern Europe was unstable, neither Germany (even democratic Germany and certainly Germany under Hitler) nor the regime of Lenin/Stalin felt secure. This vacuum became a corridor through which Soviet and Nazi troops marched and the fate of Eastern Europe was finally sealed with the August 1939 Nazi-Soviet Pact. The totalitarian regimes encircled the weak, unstable authoritarian radical nationalist illusory states.

The period between 1919 and 1939 was also characterized by the "New Diplomacy," or the diplomacy of revolution.[11] World War I became an ideological war, setting the stage for revolutionary politics and diplomacy. According to Hoffmann, quoted by John A. Lukacs:

> A war which is preeminently revolutionary in character is . . . an ideological war. It is much more than a collision between States motivated by limited purposes which can be only achieved by force. There is in it a challenge to all the world; on one side or both, there is an effort to vindicate or propagate universally an ideological purpose. The *rationale* of a better world has been revealed, and there is an apocalyptic vision of the world remade and man reborn. A militant party obtains commanding power and acts in the firm conviction that it possesses the truths necessary to the temporal salvation of mankind.[12]

The New Diplomacy would be the brute diplomacy of mass movements, not that of empires and monarchies. The most cataclysmic movements were of course the Russian Revolution and the Nazi rise to power. These events would change the nature of international politics and diplomacy for a century to come. The Russian Revolution would not have been successful without the support of the Germans or without a devastating war.[13] The Bolsheviks defeated the Cossacks, the Ukrainians, the Baltic States, and the Poles and won wars in Siberia for they understood best that these nationalities' leaders' efforts to resurrect the empire were a mistake. The Bolsheviks deceived and duped the nationalities by pretending to give them freedom, which of course was ruthlessly taken away by Lenin and his chief henchman, Stalin. Lenin was the father of what later would become Stalinism: oppression, Gulags, concentration camps, destruction of nationalities, and in the end the Stalinist destruction of his own party and its Bolshevik leadership. Thus there emerged in the ruins of the Russian Empire a ruthless ideological movement, to be rivaled only by Nazism a decade later.

What is significant about the diplomacy, politics, and war after Versailles was the Bolshevik idea that a revolution beginning in Russia could spread into the rest of Europe. The cataclysm of the revolution and the civil war created a vision among the Bolshevik true believers. They now became the masters of history, of historical materialism, and of the class struggle, the central theme of which was to destroy regimes, states, and governments.

The Bolshevik regime succeeded because of Lenin's innovation of the party state to conduct a revolution in the name of the proletariat in an essentially peasant society. In 1903 Lenin had created the first Bolshevik party. It was to be a single party which would destroy all constitutional arrangements, destroy opposition from within and without, and establish a political police state. The political police did not play a major role during the revolution and civil war but would do so under Hitler and more so under Stalin; it would be the instrument of domination and control. All permutated political institutions and structures, all social and economic movements, and all intellectual pursuits were to be dominated by the ideology of Bolshevism, which itself was represented by party domination of state and society. Political police, of unprecedented nature, would later be adopted by Hitler as the instrument of fear and of total control. The political police would help establish Stalin's so-called workers' utopia, which was to spill over the rest of Europe, mainly Germany.

The target of the Bolsheviks was of course Germany. Germany had always been the hope for all socialist and communist revolutionaries. Not only did it have the largest social democratic movement in Europe, but because it was in the process of becoming the most powerful industrialized state of the continent, it also fit Marxist visions that the proletarian revolution would prevail now that capitalism had established the foundations for its own destruction. Thus Bolshevik regimes were established in Hamburg and Bavaria and even in Hungary (1918–20). These temporary Bolshevik regimes succeeded because Germany was defeated, it had been economically punished by Versailles, and it had a large working-class movement that the Bolsheviks believed provided the foundation for a world revolution. Thus the diplomacy of revolution was linked to warfare and class struggle, and Germany in this short era of upheaval was the target of the revolutionaries. The effects of the failure of these revolutionaries would pave the way for Nazism and radical nationalism in Germany. Thus a weak democratic entity, the Weimar Republic, would have to endure the catastrophe exploited by the Bolsheviks.

Another catastrophe for Europe was the economic depression, which especially affected Germany.[14] The depression considerably weakened socialist and progressive movements, as well as much of the domestic policy of the Weimar Republic, a fledgling democracy. As much as communist infiltration and temporary communist regimes in Germany had done, the depression paved the way for the rise of another totalitarian and more cataclysmic movement, Hitler's Nazism. The literature on Nazism can fill the largest rooms of the Library of Congress and the debate over the rise of Nazism among sociologists, anthropologists, historians, philosophers, and students of radical and totalitarian movements will never cease. There is certainly no single answer to the emergence of Nazism. Was it simply the result of economic depression? Of an authoritarian and undemocratic tradition? The German authoritarian personality? Racism? Anti-Semitism? Militarism? It certainly was a combination of all, but in my view the most significant explanation for the rise of Nazism, its success, and Hitler's diplomacy and war was racism. Hitler's war was a racial war.

What is significant about Nazi rule was that, like that of Bolsheviks, it involved constitutional, administrative, judicial, racial, religious, and economic revolutionary changes. Constitutional changes in Germany began with the destruction of federalism and the construction of a centralist state. Administratively, civil service law prohibited non-Aryan (i.e., Jewish) officials from serving the national state. Important changes were made in the judiciary. The entire legal system was overhauled and all traditional concepts of law were discarded. The welfare of the state and the Nazi regime was the sole consideration, and therefore in 1934 a People's Court was established, whose function was to eliminate opposition. All political parties were abolished and only the Nazi Party was recognized. The center Catholic parties were dissolved, as were the nationalist parties that at times in the early 1930s were in coalition with Hitler. On July 14, 1933, the National Socialist Party was declared the only political party of the state.

But the most remarkable changes made in Hitler's Germany were the racial laws and the persecution of the Jews, culminating in the Nuremberg Laws of 1935, which deprived Jews of property and citizenship. In my view, the racial aspect of Hitlerism was the most significant. Hitler's war against the Jews began as soon as he came to power and would culminate during World War II, when millions of Jews were trapped in Nazi-occupied Polish, Russian, and Baltic territory. Significant changes were made in military service. Universal compulsory service was established and the army was given priorities. Hitler concentrated on the rearmament of Germany, the violation of all Versailles arrangements, and the overthrow of the Versailles regime by the re-occupation of the Rhineland, the Saar, and every German territory demilitarized under Versailles. The German government denounced all international treaties, especially the Locarno Pact, so that it could reoccupy the Rhineland and finally formed a Berlin-Rome Axis with Italian fascist Benito Mussolini in 1936.

As in the Soviet Union, these changes were coupled with great blood purges (of course not comparable to Stalin's purges, which brought an end to the lives of 20 million people and decimated all party, military, and intellectual leadership). The destruction of Roehm's Storm Troopers (SA) was an effort by Hitler to establish dictatorship and satisfy the German military, which perceived the SA as a serious paramilitary organization. Withdrawal from the League of Nations and from the disarmament conferences was part of Hitler's New Diplomacy and culminated in 1938 with the annexation of Austria, whose population was on the whole gleefully happy to see Hitler march into Vienna and played a major role in Nazi SS formations and brutalities.

Revolution disrupts the international system in important ways. The external environment intensifies the competition for security among states affected by revolutionary upheavals.[15] War becomes attractive under such conditions. We have seen the development of both the Soviet Union and Nazi Germany in the inevitable relationship between revolution and war. The movements that come to power, like communism and Nazism, threaten the security and stability of neighboring states and countries. There is a fear, which sometimes reaches paranoia, of the ultimate spread of the revolution into its neighbors. What is most dangerous about these regimes is their manic quality and belief, certainly in the case of Lenin but also Hitler, in the inevitability of their revolution and its universality. The Russian and Nazi revolutions knew no boundary because both were established on class or racial warfare. This was a universal aspiration. The inevitability and invincibility of the revolution was represented by the vast propaganda efforts to internationalize the principles of the revolution. This certainly happened in the Soviet Union with the formation of the Communist International (Comintern), whose function was to spread communism into Europe, Asia, and Africa and to support communist and other social "progressive" movements of the left, in hopes of overthrowing existing regimes. In fact, Lenin and Stalin invented this dual foreign policy: on the one hand, traditional diplomatic behavior and relationship with states, and on the other, an attempt to overthrow these regimes. The revolution alters the balance of power and intensifies security competition to improve its relative position in the system.[16] It also exacerbates security conflicts among other states.[17] The revolution opens a window of opportunity that inspires conflict among other states that seek to intervene to stop the revolution or divert it.[18]

This century cannot be defined in terms of conventional systems of autocracy, tyranny, or authoritarianism. The issue that confronted the leaders of the victors at Versailles was the reestablishment of European stability, which they failed to do. The only individual who was not on the defensive at Versailles was the American president, who made a noble and futile effort to persuade the victors of the desperate need for a liberal international order. Triumphant, unthreatened America, embodied in Woodrow Wilson, was in a position to assert a new vision. But this was not to come to fruition. Authoritarian domination, collective behavior, and political interventionist movements such as fascism, Nazism, and communism overwhelmed both the traditional balance-of-power statesmen of Europe and the idealistic American exceptionalist president. The world was not safe for democracy. In fact, the regimes that would govern the new international order after 1919 were characterized by repression, intolerance, and encroachment on private rights and freedoms of citizens, as well as the destruction of limited autonomy and of interest groups. The function of the new orders, Lenin's and Hitler's, was to politicize and bureaucratize society at the expense of cultural, social, and intellectual resources of nations. The first order, the Wilsonian, was an unfulfilled dream until 1941. Until then it was a fantasy. The other two orders sought both vertically and horizontally to dominate the international system—and they did. They established political institutions and structures for the purpose of exerting international influence. In the case of Bolshevism, this was realized through the formation of the Comintern. Hitler, who had no interest in pure international relations, would establish a racial state by means of war. For the new totalitarian systems, the international stage was set for the seizure of power and self-destruction at home and conquest abroad. Special institutions and structures were established for that purpose: political police, paramilitary organizations, and above all propaganda machines effectively backed by police and terror.

Now that the environment in which the three world orders emerged has been outlined, our next task is to examine the three competing international orders emergent between the wars and to discover why they failed.

Wilsonianism in Theory and Practice
Its Rise and Demise

WILSONIANISM DESCRIBED

President Woodrow Wilson, in office from 1913 to 1921, established a conceptual framework for American foreign policy in the twentieth century, casting a huge shadow over the foreign policies of his successors. If one closely examines the speeches and writings of presidents, one may see that much of their thinking, vision, and decision making has been based on or formed as a response to Wilsonian concepts and ideas.

Woodrow Wilson was a southerner from a defeated Confederate state. Princeton University, of which he was the president, was the most northern southern university. It was rural, it catered to gentry, and it has never had the two major faculties connected with the modern age and industrialism: a law school and a business school. Wilson represented a declining southern social class in an age of industrialists, the Rockefellers, the Carnegies, the Goulds, the age, to use Rosa Luxemburg's phrase, of capital, or of high finance. Wilson was a rational nominalist and a pragmatic idealist. He never lived in a big city, he hardly knew the automobile, and in many ways he belonged to the pre–Civil War era. Thus his orientations and public philosophy reflected this background and these experiences.

No character such as Wilson is found in the novels of Henry James and Edith Wharton, which chronicle the passing of the torch from a rural aristocracy to a financial bourgeoisie. His background, upbringing, and orientations informed him of international politics. He abhorred authoritarianism, monarchism, and above all imperialism, which represented the high stage of finance capital. This was not the imperialism of the Roman style of conquest but the imperialism of commerce. He was opposed to corporate power, financial or political, and therefore supported free trade as an economic system. He believed that free trade could correct the passion and the avarice connected to finance capital. Woodrow Wilson therefore, not unlike his later successor and imitator Franklin D. Roosevelt, was a man who was not part of his age, even if he had a profound influence on his own era. It was no accident that he had William Jennings Bryan, an agrarian fundamentalist and an isolationist, as his first secretary of state.

The only aspect of agrarian radicalism, of the rural gentry experience, that Wilson did not follow was isolationism. He was an internationalist, among the first Americans to take this view (along with his contemporary Theodore Roosevelt, with whom he shared many of the reformist ideas and the disdain for the financial elite, as well as for the emerging political power of a new class). His internationalism was different from that of Theodore Roosevelt, in the sense that Wilson was a southerner and Roosevelt was a New Yorker. We must remember that the experiences of the Civil War were still fresh in the minds of both, especially in the mind of the southerners. This aspect of Wilson, although not conspicuously evident in the work of many historians, was a major part of his intellectual makeup and had a considerable impact on his views of international politics and the world political order. He was not searching only for an American political order, democratic, exceptionalist, and so on, but also for a more peaceful, rural perception of the international system. As a southerner, he was a nationalist, not just a Confederate nationalist but an American nationalist. This aspect of Wilson expressed itself in his dealings with Mexico and Germany and, of course, in the Versailles arrangements, which will be further elaborated on later.

Wilson brought impressive, rather uncharacteristic, qualities to the presidency. He was a professor of political science, as well as a former president of Princeton University and a former governor of New Jersey. He was an extremely complex man full of contradictions. Tall, almost forbidding in appearance, he was reflective, arrogant, dogmatic, sternly Calvinistic at times, and reserved, with an unusual disposition to resort to scholarly authority and analysis of issues. One could not argue that Wilson was as great an intellectual as the Adamses and Thomas Jefferson. Nor did he have their philosophical bent. What he shared with them was grand visions, which Jefferson succeeded in fulfilling and Wilson failed. Like the Founding Fathers, with whom he saw himself filiated intellectually, Wilson considered America not only as a nation-state but as a concept and an ideal. Under Wilson, the American international ideology came the closest it ever did to absolute intellectualism.

The cardinal aspirations of Wilson's ideology fit into phrases that, although admittedly clichés, included a world safe for democracy, free trade, open borders, open diplomacy, and collective security. Wilsonian ideology rejected military imperialism, absolutist monarchies, military alliances, economic monopoly, protectionism, and other restrictive and nationalist policies.[1] It was grounded in the conviction that national self-determination is, to quote John Stuart Mill, a "prima facie" case for uniting all the members of a nationality under the same government, "a government to themselves apart."[2] Wilson's foreign policy was strongly reminiscent of that of one of the Founding Fathers, Thomas Jefferson, another intellectual idealist president who strongly believed that continental expansion could be achieved through generating commerce and trade, rather than through colonial militarist policies.[3]

Wilson's world order was to rest on an exceptionalist doctrine. As Gordon Levin has written:

> For the president, the United States represented a new departure among the nations in both a moral and political sense. With the evils of militarism and pre-liberal reaction left behind in Europe, America had an historic mission to disseminate the progressive values of liberal-internationalism and to

create a new world order. In Wilson's completely liberal ideology, imperialism and militarism were seen as essentially European phenomena associated with a past which America had escaped. In Wilsonian terms, American exceptionalism consisted in the complete triumph of liberal-capitalist values in the United States, a triumph which ensured that American foreign policy could not be guided by the atavistic values of traditional European imperialism. America was for Wilson the incarnation of the progressive future of European politics and diplomacy, after Europe had cast off the burdens of its militant and pre-bourgeois past in favor of more rational, liberal-capitalist development. The President never doubted that American liberal values were the wave of the future in world politics. Soon the whole world would follow the lead of the United States to the establishment of an international system of peaceful commercial and political order.[4]

The idea of American exceptionalism was a product of the American experience, especially that of post–Civil War America. After the Civil War, internal free commerce and the Jeffersonian ideal of the pacific nation emerged. Here were the ingredients of exceptionalism—open frontiers, pacific trade, and no standing armies, only militias. Obviously this ideology was simultaneously antielitist, populist, legalistic, and doctrinaire. It was anchored in republican ideals of individualistic liberalism at the end of the nineteenth century; it was a kind of secular religion of politics applied to the international system. It was dedicated to bringing about an end to the old autocratic and imperialistic world order represented by standing armies, courts, autocratic administrations, and subject populations. This exceptionalist doctrine heavily influenced Woodrow Wilson, whose crafting of American exceptionalism was intended to replace the world of kings, empires, aristocrats, and privileged classes with a democratic American republican and pacific world order.

What is most important about Wilson is that he was an antiimperialist regarding the American continent. It is hard to conceive of Wilson as an antimilitarist in view of his actions in Mexico and in World War I. It would be correct to argue that when it came to the Old World, the European continent, with the exception of England, he was an antimilitarist only in the sense that he opposed monarchical, imperialist regimes that were dependent on a standing military and pursued colonial policies. Wilson was intellectually and politically a utopian, whom some found naive and others deceiving. Yet his covert operations in Mexico and his attitude toward Mexicans would not qualify him as a champion of anticolonialism. From the beginning, Wilson's American international order did not seek the traditional role of becoming a great empire. It opposed imperialism and colonialism as a normal state policy. Wilson saw the physical, territorial nature of America as fulfilled—it had reached the Pacific and taken all the territory it wanted from Mexico by the time President James Polk left office. The northern border with Canada was settled in the East as early as 1812 and in the West just before the Civil War. The United States was a satisfied, continental liberal power which admitted new territories and states into the Union only on the basis of popular sovereignty. America's Manifest Destiny had indeed been fulfilled.

Wilson's internationalist order was probably a concept arrived at in reaction against imperial Germany's bristling and rampant militarism and imperialism, as well as a challenge to Vladimir Lenin and his Bolshevik revolutionary world order. Liberal-democratic and capitalist internationalism were inherently pacifistic concepts. Thus Europe and the world must end the system of alliances, military pacts, and colonialism and instead embrace American-style liberal-democratic and capitalistic free trade economic systems. There was a certain amount of self-interest at work at the point where democratic ideals met commercial considerations. For Wilson, American exceptionalism would be a model for the rest of the world; the more democracies there were in the world, the wider America's ideological hegemony would spread. A world dominated by liberal capitalism would be the ultimate shield for the American republic.

The central manifestation of Wilson's ideology was to be the League of Nations.[5] Wilson's ideas were not wholly new; he was heavily influenced by progressive internationalists, including several American liberal reformers and non-Marxist socialists. Wilson in fact had conducted a steady correspondence with numerous leading members of such groups as the American Union against Militarism, the Women's Peace Party, elements of the American Socialist Party, and various left-of-center writers for the *New Republic*, as well as with British radicals.[6] It was the Union for Democratic Control (UDC), composed of prominent British university intellectuals and pacifists such as Bertrand Russell, Norman Angell, and Ramsay MacDonald, whose 1914 manifesto would become an article of faith for Wilson.

Such a concept would require a new sort of diplomacy, one that was open and popular. Wilson's new diplomacy called for nothing less than treaties with the consent of the legislature, openly debated, the end of territorial occupation by others, the abandonment of the balance-of-power construct in favor of an international court of arbitration, peace with disarmament, the reduction and nationalization of arms industries, and the promotion of free trade by "expanding the principle of the Open Door."[7]

Wilson was influenced not only by progressives and socialists but also by conservative internationalists, who sought stability rather than change in international relations, preferring the use of international law to guarantee peace and stability.[8] Their positions harkened back to the idea of the international court of justice, the Hague, and the 1907 convention. The charter membership of the League to Enforce Peace (LEP) included President William Howard Taft, the presidents of Harvard and Columbia Universities, the British ambassador to the United States, and political scientist James Bryce, as well as other prominent Republican and Democratic Party figures. Faith in international law and arbitration bridged progressive and conservative thinking.

Events that would culminate in the League of Nations entered a decisive stage with American entry into World War I in April 1917. The new diplomacy called for peace without victory, which had a lasting and disturbing effect on conservative realistic internationalists such as Senator Henry Cabot Lodge, Wilson's great rival; Wilson was, in effect, challenging the "old" diplomacy. Wilson's exceptionalism certainly had touches of idealism, but it was not without a core of realism that would result in its forgoing the ever more elusive balance of power as a governing principle. Indeed, World War I exposed the inadequacies of the balance-of-power system. Wilson's new world order would be a system of collective security to replace balance of power through a commitment of one for all and all for one; medium and large states could all invest in a system of peace.

Was Woodrow Wilson naive? The answer is definitely not. After losing the presidency of Princeton over educational issues, Wilson entered the machine politics of New Jersey and won the governorship, turned against his mentor's corrupt activities, and then entered presidential politics as a dark horse. Not as progressive and reformist as his rival Teddy Roosevelt, he won the election after Taft and Teddy split the Republican vote. Even though he was a minority president, elected by 42 percent of the people, the success of 1912 made Wilson think he was invincible. Although fortified by his stubborn Calvinistic spirit and attitude, Wilson was one of the first American Machiavellian presidents. He may have seemed naive, moralistic, and evangelistic, yet he initiated the first American covert actions, and his interventions in Mexico in 1913 and in the Russian Revolution in 1919 demonstrate that this professor of politics from Princeton was no saint.

Of course, Wilson was not so naive as to ignore the nature of power politics in international relations. Consequently, he proposed a system for handling disputes and matters of war and peace in which groups of nations would be trustees of "peaceful settlement" motivated by pure self-interest. This policy did not deny the use of force in settling disputes, but rather asserted that disputes would no longer be solved through imperial, colonial, or annexationist arrangements between powerful states. The foundation for this policy was implemented by the creation of the League of Nations Mandate system through which former German and Ottoman colonies were mandated to the colonial powers of Britain, France, and Italy.

Wilson sought an American prescription for international

politics. This meant that if there were more democracies, collective security would enhance America's role in world politics without the need to resort to serious military commitments. He preferred a world made safe for democracy because that would also be a world made safe for the United States. Under the banner of progressive internationalism and the ideal of democracy lies a nationalist concept. Wilson implied that democracy guarantees peace. Collective security would guarantee a nonmilitaristic, nonimperial order; great powers would no longer be needed to enforce peace.

THE FAILURE OF WILSON'S DREAM

American world order cannot take place and will not survive without an American national consensus. American foreign policy is deeply linked to its constitutional arrangements, a flexible federal system, a constitution designed to respond to domestic rather than foreign needs, a foreign policy that proscribes the limits of the president's executive power, and above all, despite the Constitution's granting to the president the role of commander in chief, the fact that he is not the single source of authority in foreign affairs. He must share it with the advice and consent of the Senate, which makes it a monumental political effort to persuade Congress and the American people of his policy. Intervention must be sanctified by public opinion. It must be justified and explained to the public. American foreign policy must be communicated and marketed to the American people. It is a function of the president, to quote Theodore Roosevelt, to use the office as a "bully pulpit" to educate the American people and act as a steward of their foreign policy. Likewise, but to a lesser extent, the president needs to educate Congress. A president needs congressional consent. Wilson's failure to explain the importance of the League of Nations to the Senate highlighted this need. The president's role is fundamental in educating the nation, thereby enhancing his political capital, which extends and enlarges his authority in foreign affairs. The president's political influence as chief executive can be extended only if he can persuade Congress and the American people. Wilson paid a high price for failure to do either.

American abstention from international politics, as well as a president's failure to consult with and mobilize Congress and the American people, can lead to a fiasco. A world order must be consensual to be sustained and sustained to be successful. An American "mission" must be justified in moral, as well as strategic, terms. It has to have a sense of dedication to persuade the American public that America's role in international politics is justified. The opponent must be portrayed as an unmitigated murderer, the incarnation of evil. There can be no world order without a villain.[9]

Professor Robert W. Tucker wisely argues that Woodrow Wilson's world order was to be purchased on the cheap, that American promises to play a major role in international relations would surpass the actual commitment of resources for such an enterprise. America, distant but rich and well disposed, which had taken three years to decide to enter the war, was ideally adapted to the quartermaster role that Britain played in the French Revolutionary and Napoleonic wars: it would be the prime material supporter but a combatant only of last resort. The fulfillment of American grand promises is heavily restricted by political, electoral, and congressional support for any American initiative in foreign affairs. The best example of this for Woodrow Wilson is of course the fiasco that resulted from his intervention in the Russian civil war of 1919. Instead of an effective intervention that might have changed the course of history by defeating Lenin and communism in its infancy, the president disrupted relations with the fledgling Soviet regime.

Foreign policy on the cheap also contributed to the failure of Wilson's dream of a League of Nations. Wilson's cherished League was abandoned in the era of isolationism between 1920 and 1940 because the United States did not want to intervene politically and financially in European politics. In fact, the only areas in which the United States did continue to play a role in these years were Latin America and the Pacific.

Wilson's successors, such as Franklin D. Roosevelt, also refused to pay the price before 1945 of protecting Europe against communism. From Teheran to Yalta, FDR acceded to Stalin over the Polish question. The eventual communist takeover of Poland and Germany by 1944, before the war was over, was made easy because of the assumption that the United States was not interested in keeping its troops in Europe; President Roosevelt, in fact, told this to Stalin many times.[10] The Eisenhower-Dulles doctrine of rolling back the communists from Europe was another idea that went unfulfilled.

When was the United States willing to pay the price on the cheap? Obviously before 1941–45 and 1947–89. The defense budget of the United States when Roosevelt took office in 1933 was $1 billion; when President Bush retired some fifty-five years later, it had grown to over $300 billion. Presidential action was necessary to mobilize the nation for war and for peace, and FDR successfully mobilized the nation and its resources to win World War II. FDR's plan for an international order in 1944–45 was conceived on the basis of collective security, an orientation that was an unconscious return to American prewar on-the-cheap foreign policy. The United Nations would become the instrument of American foreign policy so that the responsibility for solving international crises would not be shouldered by Americans. The perceptive statesmanship of FDR's successor Truman and his advisers helped to create and sustain an American hegemonial and ideologically oriented foreign policy, reversing FDR's minimalist international policy. The United States extended its nuclear umbrella to Europe and built a technological army second to none, especially after the ignominious political defeat in Vietnam, that demonstrated its awesome power in the Gulf War. Even though the United States's economic monopoly has been challenged and its anticommunist mission came to a successful end, it does not seem to have relinquished its international responsibility, but again it is on the cheap. American hegemonial power is clearly demonstrated by its military, technological, nuclear superiority. This power has not shrunk and will continue to play a role, if not in American fashioning of a new international order, certainly in its ability to sustain the balance of power. President Clinton spoke of using high moral Wilsonian principles to save the people of Bosnia, yet for most of his first term he utterly failed to apply these principles. It was only after the Croats and the Serbs decided to cooperate with an American "plan" (whose future cannot be predicted) that the president intervened on the cheap. It is most probable that any serious American financial or military role in Bosnia will cease once the costs in money and manpower become intolerable to Congress and the American public.

So if Wilsonian high purpose has been the American ideal for foreign policy in this century, it has also been hypocritical; high words and principled language were not fulfilled and the American people were left with promissory notes. This would characterize American foreign policy throughout the twentieth century. The one exception to America's policy of intervening on the cheap occurred when the challenge came from a hegemonial power, the Soviet Union. Then, and only then, American manpower, treasure, and consensus were harnessed to legitimize presidential promises. This is the key to Wilsonianism—it is a doctrine of noble intentions, mainly unfulfilled by the reality of international relations.

An outstanding example of the fundamental contradictions between Wilsonian idealism and political reality is the case of Germany's future after World War I. Here, the president was forced to abandon his ideal of a new world order for the realities of power politics. Wilson failed to perceive that his traditional European allies were not new democracies but old democracies and that they were primarily concerned with the balance of power, peace and victory, and the protection of empires. To Wilson peace had to be anchored on his Fourteen Points; to Georges Clemenceau and David Lloyd George, the leaders of France and Great Britain, the German treaty had to be signed as a victorious act, not as an act of reconciliation. Punishment of Germany was the policy of Lloyd George and Clemenceau; Wilson wanted a balance between punishing monarchical Germany and rewarding a hopefully democratic Germany. Eventually, Wilson succumbed to his European allies' realpolitik, agreeing to the punitive measures his allies imposed on Germany. As argued by Klaus Schwabe, Wilson had to choose between missionary diplomacy and the realities of power. Wilson signed the Treaty of Versailles, went along with the war-guilt clause, and surrendered to the realities of power. Wilson's quid pro quo on Versailles was tantamount to surrendering his cherished hope of establishing a new world order. The president in fact surrendered to the old order and accepted the Versailles arrangements that were quintessentially anchored in the nineteenth-century concerts-of-power international system.

With regard to both peace with Germany and the Fourteen Points, Wilson tended to issue high moral promissory notes on the account of a new world order but did not help to implement these notes. He failed to encourage support for the treaty in the Senate, and therefore his ideal of integrating a democratic Germany and Russia, and eventually the Allies, came to naught. This was a great personal tragedy for an idealist, who would soon confront all the nasty realities of power—Russia turned out to be Bolshevist rather than democratic, the democratic forces in Germany struggled against domestic communists, and civil wars occurred in both Germany and Russia between 1919 and 1920. President Wilson, in the beginning, overrated the support of German liberalism and the German left and did not enhance the cause of these groups in the new Germany. He thus was left supporting traditional nineteenth-century European politics as manifested in the Versailles Treaty. The president left an unresolved dilemma: by supporting the harsh measures against Germany, he actually weakened the left-wing and liberal forces. On the one hand he accepted the harsh terms demanded by the Allies, but on the other hand he proposed an international organization as the foundation for a new world order that could not have been fulfilled in view of his decision about Germany. The German situation was a perfect case for Wilsonian democratic and liberal free trade world order, an opportunity to influence the domestic sources of a defeated Germany, to punish the military perpetrators of the war and its kaiser. Instead, he hardly rewarded the democratic forces, without which a liberal world order would be impossible.

As Schwabe concludes, "The results of Versailles were in keeping with the policies of Wilson and his advisers, policies which basically were determined by constellations of power, by domestic politics, by financial motives, and only in the last instance by ideological 'sources.'"[11] The Wilsonian peace was governed by an American mission conceived and perceived as an *American national goal* that continuously interfered with the implementation of the German peace.[12] Thus the lesson of Versailles for Wilsonianism was that the liberal world order must be led by liberal world regimes and statesmen and that a liberal America is only part of the equation. As Schwabe profoundly concludes, liberal forces in both the United States and Germany were the losers after Versailles. The economic and punitive conditions vehemently advocated by the French did not help an international Wilsonian world order to emerge.

THE LEGACY OF WILSONIANISM

Lenin, Hitler, and Wilson produced extraordinary agendas. Wilson's remained a fantasy until 1945, Lenin's was not completed by Stalin, and revolutionary Europe materialized very briefly between 1918 and 1920. Stalin's ambitions to establish a Comintern order did not come to fruition either except to dominate foreign communist powers, which failed to demonstrate any effectiveness anywhere in Europe. The best case, of course, is the Spanish Civil War, where Francisco Franco demonstrated greater resiliency and Stalin's Comintern order and his International Brigades collapsed. Hitler's order was also a fantasy that partially, and for a very brief period from 1941 to 1944, succeeded. The racial order and Nazi illusion destroyed European Jewry and much of European Russia. The fantasy that lasted longest and finally saw fruition in the second part of the century by Wilson's successors, and in that company one could include all American presidents from FDR to Clinton, was finally achieved through American hegemony after the end of World War II.

Wilsonian ideals would persist among American foreign policy makers until the end of the century, regardless of how much they were overridden by the realities of political life. American order, if not buttressed by American military power and treasure, has been demonstrated again and again since World War II to be ineffective. The reluctance to intervene massively, even though in some cases intervention might have brought about stability if not democracy, has been characteristic of American foreign policy, especially after the end of the Cold War. The reluctance to intervene has been subordinated to covert action. American presidents since Wilson have been much more effective with their rhetoric, even if it is empty, than in bringing about a new world order. For establishing a new world order requires engagement in power politics and the willingness to intervene in areas in which instability is a source of widening conflict. The paradox inherent in the new world order is that to preserve and sustain it, its creator must be deeply involved in power politics. Only in the struggle against communism, that is, the Cold War, was rhetoric combined with action. Without American weapons, manpower, and treasure, there is no alternative world power dedicated to and capable of supporting a Wilsonian commitment. In World War II and the Cold War America played a highly active role in European politics—but at the expense of President Franklin Roosevelt's brainchild, the United Nations. Balance of terror was substituted for balance of power. This world order was hardly Wilsonian; it represented power politics at its highest—yet Wilsonian principles flowed like a stream under the glacier into the next generation of presidents.

American presidents since Wilson may be categorized in two groups: those who fell under the spell of Wilsonian principles and those who owed more to Wilson's predecessor, Theodore Roosevelt. The irony of history is that the liberal Wilsonian order retreated to the Rooseveltian power politics that underpinned Wilson's idealistic world order. American exceptionalism, as I have stated, is a form of cultural and economic hegemonialism; in a world safe for democracy there must be liberal ideological domination by an anti-imperialist, anti-Bolshevik America.

Another school on America's international role in the early twentieth century challenged Wilson—the imperialist, "expansionist" group. Not unlike the balance-of-power practitioners Castlereagh, Palmerston, Metternich, and Bismarck, these writers and statesmen believed in the quintessence of the United States, but not in a narrow realpolitiker view. If the Wilsonians and neo-Wilsonians could be characterized as a liberal antiexpansionist group, this school must be characterized as conservative and expansionist. They believed in balance created by American cultural and political influence *rather* than expansion or occupation. The realist imperialists included historians such as Andrew D. White, George Bancroft, John Fiske, Frederick Jackson Turner, and the Adams brothers (Brooks, Henry, and Charles Francis), as well as Henry Cabot Lodge and Albert Beveridge. All had different philosophies, yet all subscribed to a Darwinian-Spencerist view of human and international behavior. They rejected the Wilsonian world order but nevertheless were protagonists of America's unique moral right to spread its cultural power and influence beyond the seas. They can be called the first American internationalists since Jefferson and Alexander Hamilton.

Wilson's intellectual and political rival was Theodore Roosevelt, who would become the first American interventionist president after William McKinley. Like Wilson, he was a member of the eastern political priesthood but was better known and remembered in the legend of American imperialism. This variant of imperialism held a Mahanist orientation.[13] It did not mean an aggressive land power marching to Mexico such as in 1845 or to Canada as in 1812. It meant political influence over the Pacific and deterring the emergent Japanese from occupying Pacific islands and properties. It was navalist in the sense that it was dominated by a worldview of naval service.[14] Everything was seen "through the lens of Captain Alfred Thayer Mahan," a world of Social Darwinism, perpetual strife, and racial (i.e., Anglo-Saxon) superiority.[15] For Teddy Roosevelt, the author of *Winning of the West*, "imperialism was no more than the continuation of expansionism initiated by the Founding Fathers because the targets of early expansion had never truly been empty."[16] All that followed, the acquisition of the Philippines, the Open Door Policy in China, the building of the Panama Canal, the Roosevelt Corollary to the

Monroe Doctrine, the U.S. intervention in World War I, was part of the emergent world order that has been identified with Wilson's rivals. The cases of the Caribbean, Venezuela, Cuba, Colombia, and Santo Domingo all point to Roosevelt the imperialist. But even so, Richard Collin concludes that "diplomatic expansion was but a small part of America's change from provincialism to industrial power" and that "Teddy Roosevelt was conscious of a new sense of the American world."[17] Collin argues, and I agree, that Roosevelt "seemed to exalt in the romantic notion of war, eagerly urged war as an effective American policy, and was quick to volunteer whenever a war threatened." But Teddy was no classical imperialist. He was no economic determinist, nor did he believe in economic imperialism—of which he was ignorant. He was no friend of big business, of corporations. Roosevelt "did not want colonies"; he was apprehensive of "European aggression and European nationalism and felt that the new naval technology" had protected the United States.[18] He was a boaster, a hunter, an explorer, and a racist, just as his generation's elite was culturally and socially racist. This does not qualify him to be a Disraeli, or a Joseph Chamberlain, or an Alfred Milner, all classical British imperialists. In fact, he was the complement to Wilson.

Where does Wilson meet Teddy? Both "shaped the American presidency and altered the course of politics in the United States."[19] Both were articulate interventionists. They expanded three powerful aspects of their office: "public dramatization, advocates of the people, and party leaders."[20] Wilson was more doctrinal and the other more journalistic. Roosevelt's great power was that he was a tireless evangelist for American activism, yet so was Wilson, who pursued "a more pacific vision."[21] Both believed in an American-dominated moralistic world order, but one was more prophetic and the other more realistic. Both advocated greater international involvement even if their styles and language were different. Both upset Europeans and Asians by their view of race and American exclusivity, which meant—at least to Asians—white man's supremacy. Nevertheless, their interventions in the Pacific and Latin America were perceived as realpolitik in disguise, as moral rectitude, especially in the case of Wilson. The Spanish-American War, which both defended, demonstrated their compatibility. In fact, post-1945 foreign policy would fuse Rooseveltian and Wilsonian philosophies. The fusion of American exceptionalism, vigilant leadership, liberal capitalism, collective security, and a stable market order was what the Cold War was all about. John M. Cooper Jr. writes, "Like Thomas Jefferson and Alexander Hamilton a century earlier, neither Wilson nor Roosevelt could have developed fully in his politics without the other as a foil."[22] For both, imperialism was not Joseph Schumpeter's atavistic imperialism, but rather an extension of democratic capitalism into the international system. They were democrats and nontraditional imperialists, even if both engaged in power and principle. The Cold War demonstrated that the two passions are clearly distinguished from those of European idealists, moralists, and imperialist-realists. Their worldview was uniquely American—projecting great power not to intimidate others but to offer a prescription for a stable world order.

Hegemony means that a great power's political, cultural, and military dominance flows beyond its territorial boundaries. Hegemony does not mean a great power assuming imperialist, territorial domination. In the case of both Wilson and Roosevelt, it was the sense of making the international system safe from rival hegemons—imperialist, revolutionary, or ideological—that were threatening the international system. The American hegemony paradigm involves a symbiosis that emphasizes "cultural affairs more than strategic and economic ones and looks for contextual intermediaries in a broad international perspective to help explain conflicts between nations."[23] "The big stick is a perfect hegemonic symbol."[24] It is a demonstration that perception and role-playing facilitate the hegemon, involving deterrence capability. American cultural expansion symbolically linked Wilson to Teddy Roosevelt. The ideology of exceptionalism, the high moral pitch, and the material cultural exports brought Teddy Roosevelt to Woodrow Wilson; the latter's voice was higher and the former's more ambitious. World order, American style, is symbiotically linked to American culture and American perception of what relations between nations must be. And this is why Wilson and Teddy Roosevelt have been labeled imperialist by a whole school of historians. In fact, their true successors were Herbert Hoover and FDR, both realpolitikers and cultural imperialists. The former distributed food aid to war-ridden Europe, especially Russia; the latter played an important role in enhancing the navalist ideas while he served as assistant secretary of the navy in Wilson's administration, Cousin Teddy's true representative.[25]

Bernard DeVoto argued long ago that American national and imperial frontiers are the same. This was clearly understood by Teddy and his realist associates. They sought to impose order by imagination, not by position. It was Teddy and his relative FDR who sought American power via engagement out of isolation, but this island republic between two large oceans was seeking military and naval bases, not colonial territorial assets.

It is misleading to relegate Wilson to "idealism" and T.R. to "imperialism." Both mobilized the presidency for an American international role, and both certainly were the founding fathers of American foreign policy in the twentieth century. Both were dedicated to reform in international affairs and to making it, especially in Wilson's case, more in the American image. They used their brilliant rhetoric and writings to advance America's moral role in international politics. Their legacy is clearly found in this American Century. Whereas Presidents Franklin Roosevelt, Jimmy Carter, Ronald Reagan, and Bill Clinton subscribed to Wilsonian American exceptionalism, Harry Truman, Dwight Eisenhower, John Kennedy, Richard Nixon, and George Bush were closer to Teddy Roosevelt's vision of the world. All, however, defied and refused to accept the historical European balance-of-power concept. They were neither realists nor neorealists.

AMERICAN REACTIONS TO WILSON'S ORDER

What was the conservative and progressive reaction to American foreign policy in the twentieth century? The major contrast is the absence of a call for internationalism and a retreat to American isolationist or neoisolationist orientations and ideology, except, of course, for the Pacific and South America, which have always been areas of American interest and where, in the case of the latter, the Monroe Doctrine prevailed for more than a century. The isolationist impulse came from the agrarian and ethnic population, mainly of the Midwest and the Southwest. The attitude was that Europe was the "old" country, reactionary, oppressive, and belonging to a past the immigrants preferred not to remember. The main force for progressivism in America was the Peace Progressives group, Midwesterners and sons of Scandinavian immigrants who violently opposed imperialism and American interventionism. Their targets were Teddy Roosevelt, Henry Cabot Lodge, and William Howard Taft, the neoimperialists who were influential (two became presidents) between 1890 and 1914 in America. The Peace Progressives were a block of dissidents in the Senate between 1913 and 1935, unified by the rejection of Wilsonian internationalism as well as Teddy Roosevelt's hegemonialism. They were critical of Wilson's peace and his surrender, in their view, to the old balance-of-power politics conducted by the European victors of World War I. The Peace Progressives were notorious for their rejection of power politics, but especially the role of the United States as a champion of weaker states. Led by Senators Asle Gronna (North Dakota), Robert La Follette and John Blaine (Wisconsin), and William Borah (Idaho), they wanted to make America the champion of peace and national solipsism, its foreign policy a priority for the representation of an American domestic agenda that called for noninterventionism.[26]

Following reform at home, the Peace Progressives called for a ban on commitments to western European states and for the "U.S. to employ a variety of economic, moral and diplomatic tactics on behalf of weaker states and peoples to help create what they hoped would be a more stable and peaceful international order."[27] The Peace Progressives were scions of the 1890s anti-imperialist writers and publicists, who articulated an America first foreign policy as an alternative to Wilsonian liberalism. They opposed U.S. participation in war and the enlargement of government power. The Espionage Act, for example, was an effort to increase government power over the press and public information. "Senator Borah called for prosecuting the war 'according to American methods,'" which meant "doing as little as possible to disrupt normal peacetime existence and maintaining the power of the Senate against the natural wartime tendency toward increased executive influence."[28] The liberal isolationists' alternative was to conduct a democratic peace. They were more naive than Wilson in considering the Russian Revolution a progressive movement. They bitterly opposed Article II of Wilson's Fourteen Points, which called for collective security. The United States "should mind our own business and not interfere with the affairs of foreign nations *unless it is for the purpose of assisting the weak and the oppressed.*"[29] This, said Senator Gronna, "was to equalize the weak and the strong."[30]

By the 1920s, the Peace Progressives began to eclipse the Wilsonians as the most important spokesmen for the American left.[31] They fought the military occupation of Haiti and the Dominican Republic, and their "radical anti-imperialism, unique in its consistency and forcefulness in the annals of the congressional dissent, established the Peace Progressives as important thinkers on the issue of peace."[32] They challenged Wilsonianism. A leading 1930s isolationist, Professor Charles Tansill of Johns Hopkins University, wrote *America Goes to War*, a chronicle of America's entry into World War I, and was "a vehemently segregationist southerner of Irish descent."[33] Another famous anti-Wilsonian and later a vehement opponent of FDR, Professor Charles Beard, would lead the most prolific neo-Jeffersonian attack on Wilson. Tansill, a conservative and racist, defended the work of the Peace Progressives, as did the more radical Beard. Both professors' populism targeted big business as the force behind imperialism. They conducted an agrarian Jeffersonian liberalist onslaught on Wilsonian commercial and international liberalism. Guided by this ideology, they dominated the Senate long enough to block any efforts on the part of the president to intervene in international politics. They were isolationists par excellence.

The Peace Progressives, both populist and racist, felt that Wilson's mission was detrimental to America's real interests, which were to stay at home, not to raise standing armies, and not to be involved in foreign affairs and in foreign wars. What is characteristic of this group, no counterpart of which can be found in modern European history, is that despite America's emergent economic and military hegemonialism, their ideological moorings were pacific. They failed to see that America was a world power, indeed an exceptional anti-imperialist one, and could not withdraw from the international arena, and that their type of pacifism endangered the security of the United States. This danger was clearly demonstrated by the rise of fascism and Nazism as a challenge to the West and American power that could not be ignored. The Peace Progressives and the post-Wilsonian liberal isolationists bear great responsibility for the tragedy of the emergence of Adolf Hitler. For had the United States dispensed with its Neutrality Acts policies and become more interventionist in international politics, it could have—although, of course, might not have—been able to "quarantine" the aggressors, to use FDR's word. The absence of an American willpower and an existing large-scale army provided a lesson that was later effectively learned after 1945. The Cold War was, among other things, a reaction to the isolationist era of the 1930s and the impotence of America in confronting fascist and Nazi totalitarianism.

After 1945, with Stalin's aggression, there would emerge the anticommunist liberals, led by President Truman, under whose administration American foreign policy was revolutionized. This change would be marked by the passage of the National Security Act and the creation of the Central Intelligence Agency (CIA), an independent Department of Defense, the president's National Security Council, an independent air force, and a serious nuclear and missile armaments race. The anticommunist liberals would not tolerate Stalinism and communist aggression. This, of course, led to a new mission: an anticommunist world order. This was not "new" or "old," it was unique. It was a counterideological movement of liberals who believed in muscles rather than in pacific orientations as the solution to world order. The security of Europe was preserved against Stalinism in the 1950s, based on the lessons of the absence of an aggressive foreign policy against Hitler and fascism. The liberal anticommunists were aware of the pivotal role of the Grand Republic and its imperative role in international politics. The first awakening, after Pearl Harbor, and the second awakening, in response to Stalin's aggression in Berlin and Korea, created a concerted effort to organize an antitotalitarian Western alliance to contain what was called international communism. The United States would play a pivotal role in this. Pearl Harbor triggered a sleeping giant, who since has played a dominant role based on American exceptionalist doctrine. The doctrine of anticommunism prevailed and became the bulwark against totalitarianism, represented by Stalin, Mao Tse-tung, Fidel Castro, and others.

There were two trends among the anticommunists: the liberal one (described above) and the more radical one, which was represented by several American generals and in many ways by Eisenhower's secretary of state John Foster Dulles. They called for a counteroffensive against communism. The Kennedy administration provided the momentum for such a foreign policy, but a misguided war in Vietnam and a CIA fiasco in Cuba defeated this orientation. The war against Third World revolution, first through an American effort to create "a new middle class" in the Middle East as an anticommunist force, only encouraged aggressive Arab nationalism, represented by the Egyptian military leader Gamal Abdel Nasser and Syrian and Iraqi praetorians, who still reign in the form of Syrian president Hafez al-Asad and Iraqi dictator Saddam Hussein. The U.S.-Soviet struggle in the Third World proved to be an exercise in futility for both, proven in the cases of Vietnam for the United States and Afghanistan for the Soviet Union. The Third World was praetorian and kleptocratic, and there was no hope for democracy there.

The anticommunist ideology of American foreign policy and its Cold War doctrine were challenged and became the subject of several generations of American polemicists, academics, and intellectuals. This, of course, accelerated during and after the Vietnam War. The argument was that a war meant, according to one writer, that "a powerful foreign-policy ideology has yielded unfortunate consequences."[34] These words were written in 1987, at the height of the Reagan administration. Like most liberal intellectuals, Michael Hunt considered Reagan politically anachronistic and with amazing imperception lumped Reagan's cheery faith in American strength and resilience, pathetically outdated, with Nixon and Henry Kissinger's voluptuous pessimism. The Nixon-Kissinger team, in his words, "reined in on the old ideological impulses, the 'realist' power calculus."[35] Hunt further explains the reason for this anticommunist exuberance: the American preoccupation with prestige and credibility, which was anchored in old-style anticommunism. But that was written in 1987. Only two years later, the Berlin Wall would fall and the Soviet Union would collapse. These events vindicated the *success* of what Hunt called a "powerful ideological foreign policy."[36]

The success of the Cold War, despite the Vietnam fiasco, did not demonstrate an American failure to perceive the threat of communism. It only failed to understand the linkage in the case of Vietnam between nationalist and communist forces and the Chinese-Vietnam rivalry. Nevertheless, the Cold War anticommunist ideological alliance between the United States and NATO demonstrated that the ideological vigilance of anticommunism paid off. Yes, Vietnam was a colossal error, which undoubtedly was derived from a Cold War ideology and distracted the foreign policy establishment from its real goal, the defeat of communism in Central Europe and the USSR. When the Carter administration unsuccessfully tried to traverse a different road, as did Nixon and Kissinger, to accommodate the Soviet Union, the result was Soviet aggression in Afghanistan and the Brezhnev doctrine in the Third World. The Reagan administration's unprecedented arms race and the Reagan doctrine of negotiating only from a position of strength and bringing the USSR to a status of penury certainly contributed to the collapse of the Soviet Union — even if the decay of Stalinism and post-Stalinism left the ideology and the system an empty shell. Historians, political scientists, and others will debate for a long time to come the merits of Reagan's verbal diplomatic aggression and military buildup or whether anticommunism was the major factor in the defeat of the Soviet Union. Certainly containment by treaty commitment without military deployment did not prove effective. The argument that American foreign policy was aggressive and arrogant in the era of Stalinism and post-Stalinism and that the war in Vietnam represented its futility requires an extreme straining of the sources. The anticommunist doctrine did create an American-European alliance never known before in history. Even if the Soviet Union fell on its own weight, the arms race pushed by Reagan must have helped.

The argument that the Soviet system fell on its own and that the major causes for the collapse were internal has weight. Political systems do not collapse just because their economic systems don't work. There is no question that in the military and nuclear rivalry between the superpowers and in its efforts to sustain itself as a hegemonial power, the Soviet Union gave up. In other words, the rivalry between the systems enhanced the demise of the Soviet Union. The argument that psychological containment, by itself, and "waiting it out" for this false utopia to fall was not sufficient when George F. Kennan uttered it in the early 1950s or in the late 1980s. He was wrong in both cases. Once again, military power dictates not only security, but certainly in the case of the Soviet Union the sustenance of the regime. The Soviet bankruptcy could have lasted the life of Leonid Brezhnev, Yuri Andropov, and Constantine Chernenko. But sooner or later, a Mikhail Gorbachev would emerge. Inherently the inflexibility of the Soviet system and its technological inferiority made it incapable of successfully competing with the United States in the arms race during the Reagan era.

The argument has also been made that the Reagan administration had much to do with the collapse of the Soviet Union; this is more valid than the argument that the system would have collapsed on its own. The enormous American defense budget and "Star Wars" persuaded Gorbachev to reform, the sooner the better. Without an economic engine, military power is futile. Historically and analytically, although we never will precisely prove that the Reagan administration put the last nail into the Soviet coffin, the argument may continue well into the next century. I belong to the school of realism that subscribes to the idea that naked military power without an economic base and a satisfied social system will not be maintained.

Thus in 1989 America's mission was fulfilled. The price for Vietnam, culturally, socially, and politically, was high for the United States and is still felt even two generations later. But it was not the result of a powerfully motivated ideological foreign policy. That policy was a gigantic strategic failure, whose author, JFK, failed to identify the connection between communism and nationalism. Above all, JFK and his successors Lyndon Johnson and Nixon failed to realize that Vietnam was peripheral to the Cold War. The latter wanted to extricate the United States with honor. Vietnam was also a failure of the Cold War establishment to realize the essential unimportance of the Third World to international politics. The Cold War in Asia was fought in the peripheries — Korea, Vietnam, the Middle East. But it was European recovery and Western stability and the nuclear balance of terror as a deterrent to Stalinist aggression that won the Cold War for the West. The Cold War ideology in the end, in my view, served the United States and the West so well that like the Cheshire Cat in *Alice in Wonderland* — when the cat left and the smile remained — the Bush and Clinton administrations still anchored themselves on an anachronistic foreign policy and called for a new world order.

THE WORLD SITUATION AFTER WILSON

After the end of World War I, an American leader and emergent United States could have strongly influenced the behavior of European states still guided by the classical assumptions of power politics. President Wilson, however, failed to guide, influence, or change the course of international politics when he could have done so. The president failed to distinguish between nationalism, which he believed was a liberal emancipatory force, and self-determination, which parodies nationalism. For example, the president supported the Czech nationalist claim to self-determination although no more than a third of the Czechoslovak population during the creation of the republic were Czechs. The Slovaks, finding themselves "out of the loop," resented this imposed Wilsonian arrangement and finally revolted with the aid of Hitler and established a Nazi-Slovak protectorate. The world after 1919 was not "new" at all. It may not have been possessed by the maladies of the past, but it was dominated by the infirmities of the present. This situation was highly visible in the artificial state of Yugoslavia and in the significant minorities of Czechoslovakia, Hungary, and Romania, each of which would seek freedom and independence from the state and authority established according to the Wilsonian doctrine after 1919. In the Balkans and East Central Europe, internecine and fratricidal struggles would be reminiscent of pre–World War I conflicts. In other areas, empires and colonies, which the president considered to be unacceptable in a liberal political order, remained intact, merely substituting mandates and trusteeships for historical colonialism. We know very well how "willing" and "generous" the British were in Palestine, Egypt, Iraq, and the Persian Gulf, as were the French in Indochina, Syria, and Algeria. The French bitterly fought the nationalist and independent movements of the colonial empire, thereby contributing to the emergence of Third World anticolonial and nationalist forces, which were mostly radical and supportive of the communist coalition rather than of their Western tutors. It was in these areas that Lenin succeeded in exploiting the conditions for Soviet hegemony and imperialism—all in the name of Wilsonian principles of self-determination, the political integrity of national boundaries, and the definition of the struggle of good against evil. Under the guise of Wilsonian principles, African nationalist dictators have entrenched totalitarian regimes and movements, subverting UN structures and agencies via the bloc system, and have exploited UN special and economic agencies for the dynastic enhancement of African president-for-life regimes.

The issue of bogus, high moral promissory notes would continue until the end of the century. The failure of Wilsonianism to supersede realpolitik would be experienced by all Wilsonian-oriented presidents—FDR, Carter, and Clinton—all of whom saw the realities of power dictate the shrinking, but not the abandonment, of their grand ideals. Bolshevism, fascism, Nazism, the weakness of the German left, American public opinion, the turn toward isolationism, French revanchism, and British imperialism all were realities of power politics, and all made it difficult if not impossible to continue pursuing a liberal international order.

The abuse of Wilsonianism after World War I by authoritarian regimes would be repeated over and over after World War II. A mixture of radical nationalism and fascism in Nasser's Egypt, Kwame Nkrumah's Ghana, Sukarno's Indonesia, and most recently Saddam Hussein's Iraq and Hafez al-Asad's Syria falsely paraphrased Wilsonian self-determination principles. Thus it was not democracy, self-determination, and free markets that guided the hegemonial struggle for power between the United States and the USSR, but the spheres-of-influence bloc coalition systems that competed over the Third World. The disintegration of the great Central European Austro-Hungarian Empire and the Ottoman Empire, as well as the weakening of the Russian Empire, produced only one democracy (Czechoslovakia) and no market economy anywhere between Germany and Russia. Self-determination was the powderkeg of modern nationalism, not a contribution to international stability. Nationalism and ethnicity are sources of international disorder, instigated by unfulfilled ethnic groups and nationalities frustrated over being neither independent nor sovereign.

The world after 1919 was not safe for democracy or liberal capitalism. Nor did it fail to dilute Lenin's new world order. In fact, the world that emerged from the ashes of the old precarious system of the balance of power turned out to be far more dangerous and chaotic than the world it replaced. Colonialism, militarism, radical nationalism, and revolution had preceded the signing of the peace treaty at Versailles and the creation of a new world order. What followed was an explosion of apolitical masses, the rise of the world's most destructive dictatorships led by Stalin, Hitler, and lesser personages such as Lenin, Mussolini, Franco, and Antonio Salazar, as well as other petty dictators in Hungary, Romania, Bulgaria, Greece, and Poland.

The great empires of old had collapsed, and new nations and new ethnic groups emerged, thrown together in states and territories drawn up by the mapmakers of Versailles, who seemed all too oblivious to the realities inside the borders they drew. Thus the new creations of Versailles such as Yugoslavia, Czechoslovakia, and Hungary threw together traditionally hostile ethnic groups, with one group dominating: there were Czechs, Slovaks, and Germans in Czechoslovakia; Serbs, Croats, Slovenes, and Germans in Yugoslavia; Hungarians, Germans, Romanians, and Slovaks in Hungary; Ukrainians, Jews, Poles, and Germans in Poland; and Magyars, Jews, Germans, and Russians in Romania; Turks were added to the stew in Bulgaria and Greece.

Not surprisingly, extremist movements, spurred by nationalism and old ethnic and racial hatreds, emerged in such diverse places as Finland, Estonia, Latvia, Lithuania, Poland, Czechoslovakia, Austria, Hungary, Yugoslavia, Bulgaria, Romania, and Greece. East and East Central Europe was a cauldron of nationalism, extremist, antidemocratic, and antiliberal causes ready to explode or collapse. Only Czechoslovakia would emerge as a more or less stable entity, although its very makeup would make it vulnerable to the aggressions and machinations of Hitler's Germany. In any case, it was the only genuinely democratic regime to emerge from the new nations created at Versailles, the only shining example of Wilson's utopia to survive infancy.

The world was not "safe for democracy." The prevailing order was militarism, and praetorianism tended to replace the old empires, once the principal devils for the high-minded Wilson. To be sure, there were treaties and pacts and alliances. Between 1919 and 1939, a rush of treaties were signed, none of which did much good and many of which came to be the causes or excuses for war. The Little Entente drifted toward France. They were impractical pacts. How could France defend nations that had no common border? How could France be allied with Poland when Poland and Czechoslovakia never resolved their dispute over Teschen, at least not until Hitler let Poland seize it after the Czech partitions of 1938 and 1939. The French treaty of security with the USSR strained its later commitment to Poland. None of the treaties and pacts that characterized European diplomacy between the wars were grounded in reality. They were easily broken, easily set aside as the nations geared for war and rearmed, with the singular exception of Great Britain, where military budgets actually shrank.

Not only was the world not safe for democracy, it was not safe for anybody. Territorial and interethnic disputes were fierce and were abetted by the totalitarian movements of Nazism, communism, and fascism. Totalitarianism was fanned by nationalism, not democracy or by liberal capitalism or pacifism. The reality was that the world did not return to the classic balance-of-power order, nor did it bask in the sunshine of Wilsonian democracy. Wilson's dream was quickly doused.

The two forces that tore apart the fabric of Europe after Versailles were radical nationalism/fascism and the Bolshevik revolution. Nationalism was on the march everywhere, spurred by the destructive creativity of Versailles. Would-be nationalities, ethnic groups, and religious schismatics that had been repressed during the reign of empires between 1870 and 1914 were on the rise again, replacing the old traditional authorities and class systems with populism and irredentism in the name of national and self-determination—at the expense, of course, of even weaker nationalistic groups.

The numbers were against the survival of artificially created democracies. How could Czechoslovakia survive as a full-fledged democracy, when despite its population of 24 percent Germans and 10 percent Slovakians and Magyars, the Czechs (with less than 50 percent of the population) dominated political, economic, bureaucratic, and military institutions and structures? It was a mini Austria-Hungary, a republic replacing the multiethnic empire. A similar situation existed in Yugoslavia: it was composed of 22 percent Croatians, 9 percent Slovenes, 4 percent Germans, 4.5 percent Magyars, 4 percent Albanians, and 50 percent Serbs, leaving the Serbs disproportionately dominant and the minorities seething and resentful (see Table 1). In both these cases and others, the minorities formed radical nationalist groups, first fascist, then Nazi, receiving support from Germany and Italy.

The same was true with communist parties supported by the USSR. All of these groups were mobilized to serve forces outside the Versailles frontiers. Even such distanced European practitioners of power politics as France's Raymond Poincaré and Britain's Lloyd George failed to see that illusory independence made the world particularly unsafe for democracy and instead provided the means and excuses for conflict. Postwar Europe was weak, chaotic, and insecure and therefore aggressively nationalistic. East Central Europe provided the arena for future conflict and continued instability. The independence movements dropped to their lowest common level, a condition of greedy and bigoted ethnicity, and finally fell prey to their sponsors in Germany and Italy in the West and Stalin in the East.

Gerhard Weinberg gives a vivid and accurate portrayal of Europe after Versailles: "Having accepted the principle of nationality as the basis for the organization of Europe, the victors of 1918 necessarily created a Europe—insofar as their influence reached—in which the Germans were the most numerous people after the Russians and in which by virtue of its skills and resources, Germany remained potentially a most powerful country."[37] "A united Germany might grow opposite weak, disunited powers."[38] Such a Germany would stand in juxtaposition to the weak and new states of East and East Central Europe and to revolutionary Russia.

War and revolution and the wolves of Bolshevism and fascism ravaged post-1919 Central and East Central Europe. There were revolutions in Germany and in Hungary. The peace treaties created chaos. Nationalism competed with communism; ethnics battled other ethnics, and extremist parties on the left and the right rose to the fore. As a result, by the late 1920s and early 1930s, authoritarianism had settled upon Yugoslavia, Poland, Hungary, Romania, Albania, Greece, and Austria. The vulnerability of East and East Central European states left the center of Europe prey to Hitler's Germany and Stalin's USSR.

The German revolution that erupted in 1918 was caught between Washington and Moscow. In a fair assessment by a leading diplomatic historian: "If any good could come out of the Second

World War, it would be the opportunity afforded Americans and the British to bring order out of the resulting chaos, and, in particular, to disarm all these powers who in [Wilson's] belief had been the prime cause of so many of the wars of the preceding century."[39] Even defeated, Germany remained a significant Central European power and player. In 1918–19, it was caught up in the fever engendered by the Russian Revolution. Soviet-style regimes were set up in Hamburg and Bavaria, and Soviets and Bolsheviks were battling to seize power in Berlin. In this climate, Germany was trapped between two international utopian visions, Wilsonianism and Leninism-Stalinism. Bolsheviks sought to create tyranny in Germany. In the end, the forces of Lenin were defeated by a socialist center-army coalition. The Soviet regimes in Bavaria and Hamburg were ruthlessly overthrown by reactionary forces. Meanwhile, American participation in the League of Nations was killed in the U.S. Senate, assuring from the outset that the League would be a weak and feeble force. Wilson's Fourteen Points, with the exception of self-determination, came to naught and died a silent death. The president had failed to lead his new international order.[40] Wilson lost the fight for a democratic Germany by accepting the punitive articles of Versailles. Weimar was thus left to the mercy first of the Bolsheviks and a decade later of the Nazis.

The new diplomacy was dealt a wounding blow right from the start. The redrawing of the European map had led to the rise of extremist movements of authoritarianism and radical nationalism, and these forces destroyed Wilson's hope and vision. The absence of the United States as an engaged world power was conspicuous and disastrous. The League of Nations, without the leadership of the United States, was reduced to an instrument of French revanchism and became a sounding board for struggling and conflicting ethnic groups, all laying claim to their right to the principle of self-determination in their conflicts with other ethnic groups clamoring for the same right.

In the absence of a balance of power, the rising great powers—Germany and the Soviet Union—would by the 1930s be facing each other and regarding the West with suspicion. Inevitably, they would end up dividing between themselves the weaker states of East and East Central Europe in an act of collective dismemberment of the creations of Versailles. In the 1930s, the seeds for such arrangements were sown, and Wilson's instrument for collective security, the League of Nations, was useless in stemming the growing tide.

CHAPTER 3

The Communist World Order
Leninism in the Disguise of New Imperialism

One of Wilsonianism's greatest geopolitical rivals would be the Leninist-Stalinist concept of world order. These two orders could not have been more different. Woodrow Wilson did not seek a world order that was different from Lenin's or in competition with it. Wilson was unaware of Lenin and Bolshevism until they assumed power in 1917, and even then he perceived Bolshevism to be a progressive movement. After all, anything that replaced the czar was welcome. Nor did Wilson understand that the provisional government represented progress and Leninism represented revolution. But the president would quickly learn about Lenin, his party, and his ideological, authoritarian, collectivist ambitions. Professor Woodrow Wilson had little or no knowledge about the history and evolution of Russian radicalism, or any European radical movement. The two European societies he knew best were Britain and Germany, especially the former. Awareness of British and European social democracy, especially the one in Germany, inclined the president to support such movements. He was of course unaware of the schisms that produced Bolshevism and that would represent an undemocratic, illiberal, radical revolutionary movement. The president was preoccupied with the formation of a liberal international order and with the creation and empowerment of democratic institutions. Lenin, unlike Wilson, was a quintessential Russian European-oriented intellectual and ideologue. Lenin was deeply involved in the politics of German social democracy and in Central European and Russian socialism. The United States hardly figured in his scheme. To him, the United States fell into the category of capitalist imperialism, the major representative of which was the British Empire. In a curious way, the United States was considered an extension of this empire.

Lenin's concept of a world order was Marxist, revolutionary, and socialist. Nations and societies were seen as clustered around historical and economic materialism. Class domination of the state is the oldest reality of international politics. Wilson's Christopolitical commandments were to Lenin no more than a reiteration of imperialist domination and capitalist subjugation of the proletariat. In fact, imperialism was discussed as the highest stage of capitalism. The function of a Leninist world order would be to advance communist, Marxist, and revolutionary movements in the colonial and economically underdeveloped world. International order would be consumed in the fire of war and then of revolution that would lead to a proletarian world peace. The state was nothing more than an entity of capitalist exploitation and therefore must be rejected. The mechanism to achieve this new world order would be the Communist International (the Comintern), which would support anticolonial revolutionary movements across the globe.[1] Such a world order would not be achieved by consensus, democratic means, or representation.

For Lenin, a world order, like the existing international system and all systems that required foreign policy, was to be subjugated to the interests of the Communist Party and the USSR and in fact to Lenin himself. Because Lenin's and Stalin's party was the first to achieve power, it must serve as the hegemonial party over all others. The hegemony of the Communist Party of the USSR would guarantee the success of other communist parties and movements with the same goals. Thus the Communist International was not only a reflection of the Soviet Union but also an instrument of Lenin's party and of Bolshevism. Socialist-Marxist revolutionary movements could not be trusted unless they were disciplined to follow the Leninist, and later Stalinist, principles of domination. The eventual classless society and state-less world must be harnessed for the purposes, the needs, and the aspirations of the vanguard party, that is, Lenin's Bolshevik party. This was a central theme of the Communist International, which would serve throughout Soviet history with few exceptions as the major vehicle for the creation of a Leninist order as an alternative to Wilson's. Aware of Wilson's world order and antagonistic to it, Lenin conceived his own, not only as an alternative but as the omnipotent alternative. Lenin's world order would not tolerate the existence of a competitive pretender to world order. It was a struggle for monopolistic domination of the spirit and the structure of the international system. In Lenin's view, that was the only way to achieve communist domination.

Lenin was a revolutionary, not a utopian, a ruthless and cunning leader. Both he and Wilson were critics of imperialism, that is, of the old order, as well as centuries of secret diplomacy, but their basic goals could not have been less alike. Yet the thinking and actions of both men cast a huge shadow over the rest of the century. Both men were idealists and pragmatists, but Wilson was sincerely visionary in his thinking, whereas Lenin had the laser-cold vision of a terrorist. Wilson's new world order would be formed by liberal-capitalist-democratic creeds, Lenin's by revolutionary and violent overthrow of the established order. As Gordon Levin writes:

> The world views of both Woodrow Wilson and Vladimir I. Lenin, like those of most messianic political thinkers, were centered on a dominant faith or myth. At the core of Wilson's political creed was a conception of American exceptionalism and of the nation's chosen mission to enlighten mankind with the principles of its unique liberal heritage. In Lenin's case, the central myth concerned the imminent liberation of mankind from liberalism, capitalism and imperialism through the means of a proletarian revolution led by a knowledgeable socialist vanguard. From this basis, Leninist ideology would challenge not only Wilson's ultimate goal of a capitalist-international system of free trade and liberal order, but also the

President's final decision to achieve this aim by fighting a liberal war against Germany in the interests of universalizing self-determination and democracy throughout Europe. In 1917, these two mutually exclusive visions of world history came directly into conflict when Lenin and Wilson both became, almost simultaneously, major historical actors.[2]

Despite their different reactions to imperialism, militarism, and the traditional monarchical empires and their opposing ideological positions, both Wilson and Lenin saw World War I as a war of imperialists. While Wilson meant to use American moral and economic strength in the struggle, Lenin saw the war from a Marxist perspective, as an opportunity to exploit, control, and manipulate a capitalist-imperialist struggle and divide the colonial world. Lenin, in the title of one of his most influential pamphlets, called capitalism the highest stage of imperialism. He rejected Wilson's explanation that World War I was a war between autocracy and democracy, seeing it rather as a war between rival capitalist-imperialist colonial powers.[3] As historian Arno J. Mayer writes, "Wilson counseled the allied governments to formulate liberal war aims in order to rekindle the fighting spirit of the allied masses. . . . Lenin sought to advance the proletarian revolution by convincing Europe's war-weary masses that it would be expedient to couple the issues . . . of peace with those of domestic reform."[4] Lenin saw a world dominated by finance capital, which resulted in predatory colonialism. The international relations of capitalists were by definition colonialist; that is, they were constantly searching for cheap markets outside their own environs. Taking off from the writing of social critic John Hobson (*Imperialism*, 1901) and the thinking of left-wing German social democratic Marxist theorists such as Rudolf Hilferding and Rosa Luxemburg, Lenin saw economic imperialism as inevitably resulting in war. The conflicts between imperial forces in the international arena were the major reasons for war; thus war and imperialism were one and the same. Lenin's vision of society, state, politics, and economics, and thus international politics, was based on Marxist materialistic economic philosophy. It was thus a rather antiquated conception of economic motivation that was closer to the classical economic schools of Adam Smith, David Ricardo, and Thomas Malthus than to modern economics.

Obviously Lenin's conception of imperialism was at direct odds with Wilson's concept of free trade. Foreign trade, to Marxism, is essentially capitalism, with imperialism as its highest stage. In this view, Wilson's concept of free trade is an optimistic view of the function and behavior of capital in international trade and of its beneficence.

Neither Wilson nor Lenin created his system to differentiate one from another, nor were they inspired by their rivalry. Their ideological visions coincided but were not promoted by the rivalry. The ideological divide between the two was deeper, certainly, than Wilson first realized, but the *apparent* contrast between the two systems was greater than it actually was, just as some anglers tend to exaggerate the size of the fish they catch. Yet Wilson and Lenin fished in different waters, and they tried to catch different fish. In fact, the difference between the two is like the difference between the stream and the ocean.

Lenin's world revolution began in Europe but soon expanded all over the colonial world. Lenin focused primarily on China and India and less on Africa and Latin America, areas of the world in which he had little prior interest or knowledge. Only the collapse of the capitalist-imperialist system in Europe and America could usher in the proletarian revolution. Wilson's new order meant establishing capitalist democracies where they did not exist or reestablishing them in Europe and Latin America. Lenin saw Wilson's new world order as a system dedicated to stunting the growth of his own system, especially where it was particularly promising, from his view, such as in Germany. Long before the end of World War I or the coming of the Russian Revolution, Lenin hoped Europe's largest working-class movement—that of the German Social Democrats—would join the Bolshevik Party and trigger a proletarian revolt all over Europe. He felt strongly that the proletarian revolution would take place among the workers in Germany, not in predominantly peasant

Russia, and thus his initial efforts to internationalize his revolution would take place there.

Wilson had been inspired by many voices and views, by a band of internationalist advocates which included world feminists, federalists, people like Norman Angell, Jane Addams, Bertrand Russell, and H. N. Brailsford. Lenin was heir to the great international socialist tradition that began with the First International of Karl Marx and Friedrich Engels in 1869. Lenin himself led the Third International. All the Internationals, however, involved elitist groups and were exercises in intellectual agitation masquerading as conferences. Except for German Social Democracy, there was no real mass movement or party to articulate Marxism and its international proletarian ideas. Russian social democracy at the time amounted to a coterie of loosely linked radical elites. Lenin, an authoritarian from the outset and a firm believer in the rule of professional revolutionary elites, split from the parent movement in 1903 to establish a small, militant Bolshevik group that engaged in terror and assassination. Lenin's aim was to circumvent the imperialist powers and meddle in their colonies. Beginning in 1920, he organized a campaign to support nationalist revolutions in Asia, particularly in China and India. Some can argue that here is where Lenin and Wilson met intellectually, but they adopted sharply different attitudes concerning colonies. Wilson, the liberal, abhorred imperialism, but he was not going to meddle with Britain and France and upset America's relationship with the latter by advocating the liberation of the colonies. Lenin, on the contrary, who had no qualms about severing his relationship with capitalist and imperialist states, advocated, encouraged, and abetted nationalist anticolonial revolutions. For Lenin the colonial people were soldiers in the revolutionary Marxist class and national warfare. Nationalism, which Marx abhorred, became the foundation stone for Lenin's war against imperialists. "Liberation" of former colonial people had little to do with their fate because the nationalist revolution in the Leninist world order was a step toward the making of world revolution.

Lenin created an international system in the name of the proletarian stateless, classless society, which actually was an instrument for imposing the Leninist model on the rest of the world to establish a Soviet hegemonial order. The Comintern harnessed communist parties to Soviet foreign policy, as well as attempting to subvert democratic capitalist states. In contrast, the Wilsonian order was never imposed, either on American society or elsewhere. Lenin's successor, Joseph Stalin, found a partner to help demonstrate the ineffectiveness of the Wilsonian fantasy of the exhausted democracies—Adolf Hitler. By 1939, the two of them had succeeded in destroying that fragile order, fragile because the United States was not in the League of Nations.

The Wilsonian order abhorred the Leninist one but never advocated its destruction. Of course, this mind-set would pervade American foreign policy during the Cold War, when the neo-Wilsonians and realists as well (as was Wilson)—Truman, Eisenhower, Johnson, Nixon, Reagan, and Bush—used their instrument, the CIA, to subvert communist or Marxist regimes. It is doubtful that Wilson would have condoned such behavior, and even if he would have, the Wilsonian order was not established to destroy Leninism but instead to influence the international system and bring an end to what the Leninists also thought should end: monarchy, aristocracies, and military pacts. The Wilsonians did not need to seek the end of Leninism and Bolshevism, either intellectually, ideologically, or culturally; they needed only to defend themselves against ideological and military subversion.

Another distinction between the Wilsonian and Leninist orders involved the concept of nationalism and self-determination. While Wilson championed self-determination and nationalist revival, Lenin, and later Stalin, were dedicated to the destruction of nationalism and ethnicity. This does not mean that Wilson was correct in his dogmatic championing of self-determination. After all, a state that he helped create at Versailles—Yugoslavia—has been torn asunder, demonstrating that nationalism can be a very divisive and corrosive force. Yet another distinction between the Wilsonian and Leninist world orders is the idea of collective security. Wilson's international order was founded on the premise of collective security as a way to resolve conflicts through peaceful means. It prohibits the intervention into internal affairs of states, and it recognizes without challenge state sovereignty and state independence. In Lenin's case, the opposite was true. He denied the sovereignty of states, denied the equality of states, denied the respectability of regimes that were not Marxist-Leninist, and insisted that peace derived from proletarian transnational unity, not international bourgeois harmony.

Lenin advocated and hoped for a proletarian revolution in Western Europe. He even fantasized a socialist revolution in Great Britain. The destabilization of Western European regimes by Marxist and communist parties, movements, and intellectuals was a long-lived preoccupation of Lenin and his successor, Stalin. For them, the working classes of Great Britain and Germany were the hope, actually the fantasy, leading to world revolution.

Lenin's order presumably was set to conquer; Wilson's, to end conflict. Wilson's was universalist; Lenin's was Russian imperialism under the guise of creating an international socialist community. Lenin's order was set to expand the revolutionary realm, Wilson's to expand freedom and state equality, regardless of the type of regimes and their orientations. Lenin's order was set to upset the international system; Wilson's was to bring about a wider community of states in a system of collective security. Lenin's order sought territorial expansion; Wilson's desired philosophical liberal expansion. Sovereignty and constitutional law were Wilson's heritage.

THE COMINTERN: INSTRUMENT OF HEGEMONY

The function of the Comintern was to regiment a communist world order from Moscow. The Comintern was not a combination of equal states or of equal parties and movements. It was a revolutionary organization, Lenin's instrument for world revolution and the overthrow of capitalist regimes. The Comintern and the Soviet state functioned in tandem. The Comintern was organized to subvert governments and establish communist-dominated regimes while the Soviet state engaged in traditional state diplomatic activities. Thus, on the one hand, they would subvert the system over the long run, while on the other they tried to establish an ancillary regime to the Soviet Union. The function of the Comintern was to institutionalize the world revolution and mainly to strengthen the international role of the Soviet state.

Once Lenin and Leon Trotsky were in power after 1917, they sought to establish relations between the new Soviet state and the international movement. Thus the Communist International (Comintern) was formed in 1919, headed by Lenin's party executive, the Politburo member Grigori Zinoviev. Zinoviev organized the representatives of European and U.S. working-class parties to affiliate them with the Comintern. From the start, the Comintern was a Soviet instrument to spread the Bolshevik revolution to Europe, America, and later Asia, as well as serving as an instrument of Soviet foreign policy. Internationally, its influence was marginal at best, nil at worst.[5] Nevertheless, it encouraged the rump communist regimes that emerged in 1919–20 in Bavaria, Hamburg, Berlin, and Hungary. In the 1930s, the Comintern would play a significant role as a tool of Stalin's foreign policy. The relationship between the Soviet Foreign Office, Narkommindel, and the communist nationalist parties represented in the Comintern sheds a new light on Lenin's new proletarian order.

Among the most conspicuous actions of the Comintern was its intervention in the Spanish Civil War. This complex and bitter war was a preview of the great war to come.[6] The Spanish Civil War began when elements of the Spanish army revolted against the Spanish Republic. The left coalesced with the Spanish Republican government, a noncohesive electoral coalition which played a role in the weakening of the Republic. Here, the Comintern found an arena in which Stalin's post-Leninist vision of indefinite world anarchy existed. Its purpose was to take over, dominate, and impose upon the International Brigades a Comintern of Stalinist orientation. The International Brigades, composed of communists, Trotskyites, left liberals, idealists, and antifascists, was a mixed, undisciplined group, vulnerable to Soviet machinations. George Orwell's novels on the Spanish Civil War clearly describe, in vivid literary fashion, the brutal Stalinist efforts and the Comintern's attempt to impose its policy on the disparate, idealistic International Brigades. The most vulnerable among the brigades was the Anglo-American group, a bunch of free spirits, sincere, naive, true believers, a motley of socialists and communists, some of whom fell victim to the Comintern policy. The International Brigades had little military significance but as a showpiece for the solidarity of the international left with the Comintern they had great political significance. They were "an element in the Comintern's overall operation in Spain."[7]

In the Spanish Civil War the Soviets conducted a quintessential Stalinist-Comintern operation. The International Brigades, like the communist parties and movements in Europe, were merely instruments of the Leninist world order. The victory of communism against fascism provided an appealing slogan. The two surrogate powers, Nazi Germany and the Soviet Union, played an indirect role: the Nazis and Italian fascists supplying air support to Franco, the Comintern to the International Brigades under their domination. In the same vein, the Comintern tried to subvert the Spanish Republican government. Thus the experience of the Spanish Civil War nakedly demonstrated the machinations of the Comintern and of Stalin.

Once Stalin had achieved mastery, the Comintern redirected its efforts to winning in the socialist and democratic camps. As soon as possible, the Soviet commissar of foreign affairs, Maxim Litvinov, launched a massive campaign for collective security within the League of Nations and outside of it. The Soviet Union signed security treaties right and left, including ones with France and Great Britain. It gained American recognition in 1933, which greatly enhanced its capacity to infiltrate America's intellectual and progressive circles and camps. Litvinov's collective security blitz was linked to the Popular Front.

THE POPULAR FRONT

Domestically, Stalin, who emerged as the Soviet Union's unrivaled leader by 1927, set out to destroy, purge, and annihilate all opposition, including the old Bolsheviks and his opponents, real or imagined, in the military. The result was purge trials, the annihilation of the rich middle peasantry through imposition of a ruthless system of collectivization, and the starvation of the Ukranian peasants. Socialism also institutionalized the Stalinist totalitarian state. Beginning in the early 1930s, a new foreign policy strategy was designed for the Comintern which was effective only in directing national communist parties in Europe, the United States, and Asia. The Depression and the rise of Nazism presented opportunities for Stalin and animated him to revive Lenin's idea of revolutionary world order, this time under the guise of United or Popular Fronts. This meant changing Lenin's overtly hostile policy toward socialist and democratic parties and movements and intellectuals and instead trying to co-opt or infiltrate them. The main effort was now directed toward the establishment of communist fronts with socialist, democratic, or communist parties everywhere, from Europe, to China, to Asia and America.

The rise of Nazi power in Germany and the Great Depression in Europe and America served the purposes of Soviet propaganda and infiltration in Europe. The Great Depression produced a significant group of American and European intellectuals and fellow travelers that the Soviet Union and the Comintern could depend on. It seemed to intellectuals in the world of the 1930s that the Marxist prophecy of the inevitability of the collapse of capitalism was coming true, and the logical alternative would be a communist order. Hitler and Nazism offered Marxist and communist intellectuals and their fellow travelers the hope that capitalism and imperialism would collapse: out of the crucible of the Depression and Nazism would emerge a new communist world order. In Moscow the conditions of the late 1930s were perceived by Stalin and his Comintern lieutenants as providing a propitious opportunity to spark the Leninist world revolution. The communist spy network in Europe and the United States was to complement the Comintern's popular frontism. The spy network, however, was totally dominated by Stalin's secret service, the NKVD, which oversaw the Comintern. Thus the hope was that the "inevitable" Marxist proletarian world order mobilized by true believers in a network of spies would bring an end to imperialism and become the first stage of the proletarian revolution.

It was not a well-conceived military and strategic plan. It was nevertheless a conspiratorial effort that extended Stalin's power beyond the borders of Mother Russia, the USSR. The Marxist intellectuals and fellow travelers, however, were governed by a strategy and ideology that produced a plan for accomplishing world revolution. The intellectuals, especially fellow travelers, paradoxically were more conspiratorial than Stalin himself. Not that Stalin ignored or failed to exploit the duped and well-meaning Western intellectuals, especially since they offered their services to the Comintern and the revolution willingly and passionately. Stalin would hardly be in a position to refuse their assistance. Therefore, in the 1930s the intellectuals became the soldiers of the revolution and their masters in the Comintern and the NKVD their captains.

The Popular Front was a strategy adapted by the Comintern and Stalin to help manipulate the international policies of European powers through the use of working-class parties and movements. Popular Frontism involved renewed efforts to inject communist ideology, propaganda, and structures into the socialist or democratic parties in particular countries. This was done through the infiltration and the use, under Stalin-Comintern sponsorship, of communist organizational techniques: support groups, the infiltration of the Western press, and propaganda instruments to help overthrow democratic or established governments by peaceful means. A spy network was established to mobilize noncommunists to Stalin's cause.

Stalin created a new international order to establish Soviet hegemony. It called for political coalitions between communist and working-class parties, a complete turnabout from Lenin and Trotsky's policy of hostility toward fellow socialists. The interplay between socialists, Soviets, and communists, characteristic of the Popular Front, was anchored in the diplomacy of the 1930s and would play a pernicious and dark role in the Spanish Civil War. Ironically, in the meantime the Popular Front was enjoying great popularity, especially in the United States, at least in part because many intellectuals there saw the Spanish Civil War in idealistic terms. The Popular Front had its biggest success—for a time—in France, when the French Communist Party (PCF), led by Maurice Thorez, a key Comintern figure who affected Popular Front policy when he joined Léon Blum's 1936 Socialist-led government coalition, created the first Popular Front government in Europe. Defeat in Spain two years later brought about an end to Popular Frontism. But in 1936, it was Stalin's greatest success to see a Communist Party in a French cabinet, which immediately led to aggressive infiltration of the French bureaucracy.[8] The PCF was instrumental in recruiting for Stalin's and the Comintern's International Brigades to defend the Republican regime in Spain against Franco. This would lead to a Stalinist purge of the brigades, which in turn gave Hitler and Mussolini even more of an excuse to intervene in Spain on a highly visible, active military level.

Popular Fronts and movements were launched internationally. These fronts would be called "friends of the Soviet Union" or other innocuous-sounding names. Propaganda would be aimed at the soft underbelly of liberal and socialist movements in Europe as well as the anticolonial nationalist movements in Asia. As Stephen Koch wrote, "Anti-fascist committees sprung up all over Europe and in the United States. Women, youth, other liberal, and Soviet groups were infiltrated under the banner of anti-Fascism, a world-wide peace campaign was conducted. This was a joint campaign against imperialism to impress parties in India and China." Workers' organizations, unions, intellectual groups, and broad structures of the West were infiltrated by the Comintern. An Orwellian system of spies and writers was exploited to serve the secret Soviet war of ideas against the West. Lying for the truth was organized by Stalin's agent Willi Munzenberg, the Comintern's version of Joseph Goebbels, a German communist propagandist who created a unique network to control covert and innocent fellow travelers and left and progressive sympathizers, making them into "right-thinking non-communists."[9] Such famous individuals as Albert Einstein, Ernest Hemingway,

Theodore Dreiser, John Dos Passos, H. G. Wells, Romain Rolland, and Pablo Picasso were recruited, sometimes unwittingly, to various causes promoting international peace or enlisted to speak at anti-imperialist conferences. Of course, the rise and threat of Hitler stimulated in perverse fashion the interest of creative people on the left. As a result, the arena for infiltration widened under the effects of the brilliant and subtle propaganda strategy of Willi Munzenberg. Arthur Koestler was for a time in his employ before he saw the light and perceived the "darkness at noon."[10] Groups such as "Workers against Fascism" and anti-fascist committees sprung up, all run by Munzenberg and his Comintern cronies. The appeal of Lenin's proletarian, stateless world in the era of Hitler was revived, refined, and spread under Moscow's control.

STALIN AND HITLER: PARTNERS IN THE DESTRUCTION OF WILSONIANISM

The Leninist world order was established to wage a struggle against the international order, and this struggle was vigorously pursued by Stalin when he colluded with the dedicated wrecker of Versailles, Adolf Hitler. Between the two of them, they ended the Versailles order, President Wilson's pet project. The absence of the United States from the international system had weakened the League of Nations and created ample opportunities for the two ideological and radical dictators, Hitler and Stalin, to divide among themselves the "vacuum" between Russia and Germany, that is, East and East Central Europe. Without the support of the United States, the Wilsonian collective security order was of no great value.

Stalin's quintessential effort would be his drive to the West that began with the Nazi-Soviet Pact of 1939, followed by manipulation of his wartime allies, the United States and Great Britain, at Teheran and Yalta, and finally by the establishment of a communist world order between the Vistula and the Oder-Neisse. Stalin's relentless, despotism-fulfilling drive to the West— his *Drang Nach Westen*—was one of the most important and illuminating acts of the dictator's ambitions and those complicit in fulfilling them to emerge before the beginning of the Cold War. Not incidentally, it also squarely lays the blame for the causes of the Cold War at Stalin's doorstep and shows that he would not have wanted it any other way.[11]

Stalin went about fulfilling his design to occupy and "stalinize" Poland and especially Germany, his key target in Western Europe, as well as the other Eastern European Stalinist satellites, with the help of his organizational henchmen, German and Polish communists in exile in the USSR since the rise of Hitler. Yet these were merely the human instruments with which to execute his grand design. Stalin had bigger help from his partner in crime, Adolf Hitler, and, sometimes unwittingly and sometimes not, the Western allies and appeasers, ranging from Neville Chamberlain and the French in the 1930s to his wartime allies Franklin Roosevelt and Winston Churchill.

The story then becomes a multifaceted one of collusion first between Hitler and Stalin, then of collaboration between Stalin and those he deceived in the West. Hitler and Stalin were opposites in almost every way and certainly schemed to destroy each other, but they shared one common and critical goal: the destruction of Versailles and the post–World War I European international system. In this, the two dictators succeeded. A leading scholar contends that the secret agreement between Hitler and Stalin and the 1939 Nazi-Soviet Pact which followed was only the first step of a consistent Soviet *Drang Nach Westen* policy that would eventually come to fruition in 1944–45. As R. C. Raack states, "The wartime disputes between Stalin and his western allies originated over nothing less than the redisposition of the territorial and governmental results of the Nazi and Red dictators' original territorial deals."[12] Raack's analysis amounts to a serious rebuke, if not an indictment, of Roosevelt and Churchill for cleaving to their World War I experiences and ignoring warnings and advice from experts who said that Stalin was no true ally but a convenient war partner who had his own agenda, which ran counter to Western postwar purposes and policies.

This point of view runs counter to long-standing misconceptions that denied or ignored information about what Stalin really did and what his goals were and led to the popular and guilt-ridden notion that the Cold War was a Western invention: creation at worst, or an accident at best. These theories suggest that the Cold War came about as a result of Western policies, whereas in truth, as Raack notes, "Stalin himself hardly could have wished for a different outcome."[13]

Stalin was the heir to Lenin's claims to authenticity, politics, diplomacy, and ambitions, and he succeeded where Lenin had failed in the pursuit of "Lenin's radical domestic and international program."[14] The Lenin-Stalin effort was more than a Russian program; it was the raison d'être of the Soviet state—the march to the West to establish a Soviet international order in Europe. This was a clear case of hegemonial aspiration.

Both Stalin and Hitler were obsessed with a single goal: to overturn the European and Asian world order. Stalin, then, had everything to gain, as Lenin thought he had in World War I, by encouraging every possible imbroglio between Germans and the Western allies.[15] Hitler's amazing adventurism handed Stalin a highly favorable, if potentially dangerous, diplomatic tool in "the prospect of a general European war": the Soviet-Nazi Pact.[16] Hitler's offer, as the cunning of history would have it, could "set the spark to ignite the flame of world revolution."[17] Far from trying to avoid it, Stalin encouraged the coming of the war to the West. He did not do this, as Western historians would have it, merely to defend Russia from Germany. Stalin was not a gambler by nature, but he was single-minded in his goal of "fulfilling world revolution," which meant Soviet supremacy in Germany and thus the West.

Between them, Hitler and Stalin finished off the Polish state before coming to grips with each other. They accomplished this by taking a Western perspective, rooted in the experience of World War I, which caused FDR to view the Soviet Union in "a far more favorable light than he wanted to cast on Hitler's Germany."[18] In 1939, Stalin had gone a long way toward executing his Western strategy by joining Hitler "in the destruction of Europe's pre-war order."[19] The end of the new Baltic states was in sight, and Poland was next. That task was completed in 1940, when Hitler and Stalin split Poland, with eastern Poland becoming a Russian colony, and later, at Teheran in 1943, with the connivance of FDR and Churchill, who seemingly acquiesced to the formation of Stalin's state in Poland at the end of 1944. All of this happened before the war was over, through Stalin's deceiving Churchill and FDR. The Red Army would ultimately "liberate" Poland and deliver it to Stalin's Moscow henchmen. Behind the Red Army lines, the army, NKVD units, and vengeful moles rounded up and killed Polish civil, political, and military officials, completing a task begun by Hitler.

Polish carpetbaggers would become the tools of Stalin's Red Army–NKVD regime in Poland. Large numbers of the Polish population were systematically deported between 1941 and 1945. Western leaders, although aware of Stalin's encroachments in Poland, chose for political reasons tacitly to accommodate Stalin at the expense of Poland. They made assuring noises about promises of "good behavior" on the part of the Soviets, although Churchill would in the end recoil. Raack concludes: "In any case, Churchill's conditionless pledge of British aid to the Soviets, and British fears of a Soviet withdrawal from the war, blunted whatever might have come from any subsequent efforts to get Stalin to agree to restore the status quo ante bellum in Poland, or anywhere else. Later, Churchill and Eden did make occasional frantic efforts to restore the London exile government, or part of it to Warsaw, but they never supported its efforts to regain its Soviet-annexed territories."[20] For far too long, both FDR and Churchill continued to believe in Stalin's "reasonable understanding and willingness to limit Soviet self-interest."[21]

As early as 1937, Stalin had planned his march to the West, and the Nazi-Soviet Pact of 1939 was a first step toward the culmination of that plan, which was largely successful when the Red Army marched toward the West during the war. Germany was the key to Stalin's goal, "the keystone of a future Bolshevized Europe."[22] The Red Army and the NKVD police would coordinate with the German Communist Party in Moscow, exiles who had been planning a return since 1937. Taking advantage of Western wartime goodwill, Stalin was playing a significant role in determining the future of Europe as his armies advanced to the West. With Walter Ulbricht, "the real leader of the group of survivors of the Muscovite leadership of the pre-war German Communist Party," in the lead, the plan followed its course, culminating on the day Ulbricht disembarked from a Soviet plane behind the lines and was transported by a train not far from Berlin.[23]

The design was premeditated and clear—to create a Soviet fortress in the heart of Europe with Germany as the springboard. Stalin thus managed to exploit wartime cooperation with the West. As Raack noted,

> We know considerably more about Germany because its former Soviet Zone Communists over many years proudly published so much of the early history of the "republic" they designed in Moscow and then created from central offices in the eastern sector of Berlin. Their newly opened archival sources make clear how closely Moscow controlled their enterprises: that is to say, Moscow gave them direct orders through the Red Army NKVD as Stalin gave the Poles direct orders through his picked leaders in the PKWN. The German Communist party leaders had agreed in advance to do as they were told (Wilhelm Pieck had, after all, publicly lauded Stalin as the father of the Soviet people and of progressive mankind). The campaign that culminated in their open assumption of power in the eastern half of the former Reich capital, and in the Soviet Zone of Germany, ultimately became the central point of public attention in this central, post-war Western Allied-Soviet meeting. Berlin, starting in 1945, was to become the dramatic focus, and the main symbol, of the Cold War.[24]

Thus, "quietly, well beyond the eye of the camera, Ulbricht and others had earlier set about the tasks for which they had long prepared."[25] With the tight control system engineered by the NKVD and the Red Army before the fall of Hitler and Berlin, the German Democratic Republic came into being. Yet this deception and conspiracy could not have been accomplished without at least the tacit, if not open, knowledge of the West and its victorious armies and generals. The leaders, statesmen, and generals of the democracies, especially FDR and Churchill and their array of diplomatic and military advisers, consistently misled their own people and the Germans, not to mention themselves. They continued to delude themselves into thinking that "Stalin would now conduct himself like a responsible and moderate leader of a nation that had been an ally."[26] Neither FDR nor Churchill was particularly gullible, but FDR was desperately intent on acquiring Soviet help and cooperation after the war, and so he arrogantly, ignorantly, and carelessly persisted in his pursuit of Stalin, which resulted in disinformation and subterfuge galore. Stalin himself was a master of such tactics, and he used them effectively on the West.[27]

Stalin's territorial plan was probably fixed before Yalta, certainly by the time of Potsdam. He pursued his grand design, "unilaterally established central governments in Bulgaria, Hungary, and Austria and was pushing the Western allies to accept them."[28] He used disinformation and benign-sounding and stirring words like "democracy," "freedom," "antifascism," and "socialism," while avoiding the use of the word "communist,"[29] for a basically gullible Western press, while remaining true to his "consistent plan."[30] Raack describes Stalin's methodology:

> It was a consistent plan: no information, or misinformation, or disinformation, all to the end of creating a dark pall behind which Stalin could work out his purposes for Germany, and for all of Europe, in the late spring and early summer of 1945. The idea was to keep matters as flexible as possible, and to keep the Western allies distracted, while keeping political partisans of non-Communist persuasion uninformed and off guard, allowing Stalin to make the maximum possible in claims and advances and to take full advantage of the chaos he had helped to create.[31]

The role of the West in appeasing first Hitler and then Stalin remains one of the most remarkable and frustrating stories of this century. Equally remarkable is the cooperation between Hitler and Stalin in their determination to destroy the post–

World War I European order. Once the Soviet Union had become an ally and the object of an invasion by Hitler, Western leaders continued to ignore Stalin's grand design, which he had never abandoned. He never wavered in his scheme to spread revolution and Bolshevik control across Western Europe, and this the West failed to acknowledge until it was almost too late.

By the time of Potsdam, the veil was finally lifted from the eyes of the West. According to Raack:

> The evidence of Soviet deceptions and the Soviet state's different political and social values fell steadily into place at every level and locale of Western Allied-Soviet encounter over the summer of 1945. The Westerners saw for the first time, at first hand, the giant propaganda banners, the posters with their blown-up and retouched photos of the vozhd and his Kremlin subalterns, the oversized signs and symbols expressing Soviet power handing everywhere among the ruins of Berlin, doubly absurd in the ravaged landscape. These were the standard Soviet trappings, long familiar in the Soviet homeland and soon familiar in the vaster empire, but, at the time, strikingly new to the West. . . . The Westerners were astounded, too, by the newly put up, obviously permanent victory monuments and memorials, all of which proclaimed the magnificence of the Soviet victory, the power of the Soviet armed forces, the grandeur of Soviet leadership, and the eternal correctness of its thinking. All stood out against a background of complete disaster.[32]

At Potsdam, the new president, Harry Truman, and the new prime minister, Clement Attlee, neither of whom felt burdened by FDR and Churchill's Teheran and Yalta commitments, defined the limits of "further Soviet encroachments."[33] The evidence of Soviet deception became apparent and impossible to ignore. Protective diplomacy now took the place of utopian hopes. The West "had to define a limit to further unilateral Soviet encroachments."[34] But this did not deter Stalin. Unimpressed by the vagueness of Potsdam's finish, while Truman and Attlee rushed home to attend to domestic affairs, he continued to further his plan to defy the West with his "expansionist ends." Thus was triggered Truman's response to Stalin's provocative actions, making Stalin the father of the Cold War.

In conclusion, Stalin, in the old nineteenth-century balance-of-power tradition, saw the future of international politics and Europe in a totally different perspective and with different strategies than Roosevelt and Churchill did. Their worldviews were asymmetrical and in the end irreconcilable. So he could collaborate with Stalin, Roosevelt designed the policy of the marginalization of Europe to promote peace and U.S. interests.

CHAPTER 4

Nazism
The Racial World Order

Adolf Hitler's Nazi regime (1933–45) was dedicated, as was Leninism/communism, to the establishment of a new world order driven by ideology and in the national interest. Hitler's new world order was to be a racial world order, a racial utopia.[1] Hitler's racialism was a tool to replace the old balance-of-power order, which had collapsed after 1918, with German hegemony over Europe. But this order was never as broadly based in the international scheme as those of Lenin and Wilson. Wilson sought to establish a moral American liberal-capitalist international order using the American-inspired League of Nations; Lenin's Comintern would be the headquarters of Russia's Soviet international order. By its very nature, Hitler's racial utopia was restricted to one people, or at least one race, one regime: the Hitlerian Nazi regime. Whereas Wilson and Lenin espoused internationalism from the prism of Washington and Moscow, Hitler's order and ideology had no Comintern, no League of Nations.

Stalin's penetration of and infiltration into "capitalist" and "colonial" regimes were conducted by clandestine means by the Comintern, the communist parties, and fellow travelers. The effort to subvert capitalist colonial governments was proclaimed, of course, as progress, socialism, and egalitarianism, a social utopia. Hitler had no use for a Nazi international. His methods were directed toward fulfilling his racial order by conquest. He had no fellow travelers, nor did he seek them. He of course exploited the desires of German minorities to reintegrate with Nazi Germany. And even in the notorious case of the Sudeten Germans, they pressured Hitler to bring about the breakdown of Czechoslovakia in 1938. His claim to "liberate" minority Germans was phony. In March 1939 he occupied all of Czechoslovakia, hardly a state populated by a majority of Germans. Hitler's strategy was naked conquest and occupation. There was nothing clandestine about it, nor did he intend to establish a Nazi-oriented Comintern. In fact, Nazi parties in Europe—in France, the Balkan States, and Greece—were mostly ignored by Hitler when he occupied these countries after 1939.

Stalin's methods were cautious, linked to a methodical psychological and intellectual penetration and subversion of regimes. Hitler's theory of racism held that Germans were superior to all other races. His racial world order was clearly divided into inferior races to be colonized like the Slavs, superior races like the Anglo-Saxons and the Scandinavians to become partners. The only race targeted for annihilation was the Jews. About the concept of race, Theodore Hamerow writes, "Essentially, that concept meant anti-Semitism. For behind all the theorizing by the Third Reich about racial differences, and behind all the pseudoscientific lecturing on the distinctions between brachycephalic and dolichocephalic types, between Nordic and Mediterranean peoples, between Teutonic and Slavic characteristics, between Occidental and Oriental mentalities, and between the white and the colored races, there was only one fundamental principle that remained beyond debate or compromise: hostility toward Jews."[2]

Race was a biological concept. It was hierarchical and exclusivist. Proletarianism was a social and economic concept. It advocated egalitarianism in contradistinction to Hitler's racism. Both Nazi and Soviet concepts were programmatic, striving for an egalitarian or racial international order. Both were revolutionary ideas, both called for violence and destruction of the international order after Versailles, and both targeted the overthrow, by subversion or conquest, of democratic and liberal societies and regimes.

Leninism and Hitlerism were metaphorical brothers in the same uniform in being visions that forbade any but tactical constraint. There not only could be, but must be, nothing short of total triumph and total destruction of the other. Wilson and Lenin used ideology as a weapon of influence and penetration to fulfill their vision of world order. Hitler's severe ideology all but precluded the use of influence to attain fulfillment; it *necessitated* the use of force to impose the new world order because Hitler's international order could be achieved only by destroying the competing orders, Bolshevism and democracy.

But despite the obvious differences, Lenin and Hitler used similar methods. Both exploited ideas; both were driven by ideologies of conquest and destruction. Their international order in the end would be achieved only by violence, as opposed to Wilson's idealistic call to exceptionalism and democracy. Both systems would end up engaged in wars of annihilation, eventually facing each other in a cataclysmic war that seemed inevitable because of their pursuit of their individual world orders.

Nazi racial theories were not unique but had their origins in Social Darwinism, racial hygiene, and reconstruction theories.[3] The rise of science, the crisis of industrialization, and a burst of intellectual freedom had turned science into an ideology in the nineteenth century, and Darwinism only reinforced the ideology of national integration. Evolutionary biology offered an "objective" criterion for evaluating "fitness."[4] Darwinism and German culturalism would have tremendous and unforeseen political implications and consequences. Liberal and nationalist political parties were influenced by Social Darwinism, and their concerns about the degeneration of the population at large enabled the concepts of race, which had hitherto been the exclusive domain of right-wing parties, to gain popular respectability and acceptance.[5] The concept was tied to national agitation and brought on the emergence of Darwinian demagogues who would play a role in proletarian and Nazi ideologies a century later.[6]

The liberal Alexander von Humboldt of *Kosmos* fame held "the expectation that biology was internationalist, popular, and respective of other races and cultures." His writings, not surprisingly, would be condemned by the Nazis. In fact, the most respected Darwinists of the day were Ernest Haeckel and Rudolph Virchow. Haeckel became the most virulent propagandist for hierarchical and authoritarian politics, supporting the idea of a *Kulturstaadt*. He sincerely believed in selective breeding along racial lines.[7] He advocated the elimination of imbeciles and wrote of "central races" and "anthropological racism." "All the weak, sickly, or physically deficient children were slain," Haeckel wrote with a tone of approval, describing the Spartan model, which he obviously admired. "Only the children who were completely healthy and strong were allowed to live."[8] The scientist Willibald Hentschel advocated the creation of "stud farms" where men would be selected according to racial criteria. Some of the thinking of Haeckel and Hentschel would show up in the Reich—breeding farms, sterilization, and the elimination and murder of retarded children. Their influence was strong among the Nazi ranks—especially Heinrich Himmler, the head of the SS, Walter Darre, and Rudolf Hoess, the commandant of Auschwitz.[9]

The key idea that took root in Social Darwinism was the racialization of anti-Semitism. The idea of a separate Jewish race had its origins in German liberalism and anthropology from the beginnings of the Bismarckian Reich in 1870. The rival professors Eugen Dühring, Wilhelm Marr, the father of modern anti-Semitism, and Adolf Stoecker, the leader of the racist, anti-Semitic Christian Social Party were influential ideologues who were idolized by Hitler and from whom he took many of his ideas. They advanced anti-Semitism as a racial, political, and ideological doctrine which anticipated Hitler and the Nazi regime.

The impetus to prevent racial degeneration would exploit anthropological, biological, racist anti-Semitism, a combination that was itself degenerate. The idea of a utopian, racist blood Bund, in effect a German world state, was advanced by no less a personage than the Reich's minister of science and culture. Oaths of blood in schools and concepts of racial purity took on respectability and became a part of accepted political and ideological currents and thinking.[10] The *Jugendbund* had among its adherents Jews, Poles, and Socialists, who, for purposes of collectivism and social organization, called for state social engineering that paradoxically aped and complemented the thinking of the anti-Semitic racialists. So did so-called sanitary utopias.[11] Hitler's *Mein Kampf* is replete with racial anthropological hygienic and anti-Semitic theories—brutally and inelegantly stated.[12]

Racial hygiene was linked to Hitler's concept of a new Europe, a new order. Germany must cleanse itself of non-Aryans and impose a concept of racial selectivity over German-occupied Eastern Europe, which for the most part is non-Aryan and therefore inferior. War was considered a racial purifier, the tool for the creation of a new international order guided by the leading racially pure state of Nazi Germany. According to that thinking, the French, whom Hitler despised, were *not* considered an inferior race. Slavs, however, most certainly were. What Hitler was proposing all along was war in the East. Hitler was genuinely surprised when Britain, which he saw as a kindred Aryan state, went to war over Danzig. The war Hitler had really wanted and desired was one in which he could establish a racial world order over the inferior Slav races in the East, as well as the Jews, who of course had to be eliminated altogether. A new world order would be established based on the *primacy* of race.

In that Nazi theology, the leading European race was the Aryan race, which included, in addition to the Germans, the English, the Anglo-Americans, and the Scandinavians. The destiny of Hitler's Reich was to subdue, enslave, and exploit the inferior European races, the Slavs in the East. The hierarchy would remain fixed and immutable. There would be no education, mobility, or wealth for the racially inferior groups. Above all else, the Jewish-Bolshevik-Slav Hitlerian racial-ideological combination would not be allowed to survive in any form. Conquest, unfolding into occupation, slavery, labor camps, concentration camps, and finally gas chambers would eradicate the "viruses" of inferior races, first through enslavement, then through elimination.

The most natural targets for elimination were the Jews. The Jews did not even merit the status of slaves, which was reserved for the Slavs. Here another racial-hygienic concept comes into play, that of *Mischelung*, or miscegenation. In this concept, the Jewish race is a pollutant attacking the Aryan race like a virus, and therefore it must be eliminated. The concept is that there is no room for mobility in this nightmare world of race, no way to change one's status. Birth is a biological fact that sets the infirm apart from the superior race. Inferior races are biologically doomed and potentially dangerous because of their infectious qualities. This echoes Haeckel's idea of eliminating imbeciles so that they can never inbreed and weaken the society as a whole. So, too, must the Jews be eliminated in this new international order. Michael Burleigh and Wolfgang Wippermann conclude: "The Volkish state had race as its central value. It was essential to maintain racial purity because inbreeding between races caused degeneration of the higher race."[13]

Hitler elaborated and modified and added to his distinct nationalist-socialist ideology of a Volkish state and international system based on the purity of blood and race. At home, social science, medicine, and eugenics could be put in the service of the state to cleanse society. The new international racial order would exalt the German race and defend it against the inferior races.

Critical in this concept is the idea of *Lebensraum*, or living space, a geopolitical doctrine of conquest married to the racial base of the Volkish state. In this world, the higher or Aryan races are meant to exercise domination over the inferior races such as the Slavs by occupying their lands and enslaving them for the purpose of maintaining the higher standards of the superior race. Mastership all but dictates spatial expansion. This meant the vast region of the East from Poland to Siberia would become a slave state and breadbasket, an endless supply of resources for the Aryan race. Hitler greatly admired the British Empire in which he saw his Aryan brothers dominate and exploit black-, yellow-, and red-skinned races. He envisioned an association of the great Germanic state.

The dilemma for a racial world order is that while Marxism and democracy were internationalist or supranationalist ideas and movements, a purely Aryan or German ideology could not become internationalist in scope. The Hitlerian concept of a new racial world order could not be fulfilled except through war, conquest, occupation, and enslavement. Whereas Wilson espoused the integrity of all nation-states racially equipped for democracy, Hitler's new world order stopped at the borders of Germany and Austria, or at best with states that had German minorities such as Poland or Czechoslovakia. Even in Germany, the new world order was never entirely a voluntary system but an imposed one. It was a system that had to be rigidly enforced and policed. Racial legislation, institutions, literature, and propaganda were established in the occupied Eastern territories.

Norman Rich wrote that as early as *Mein Kampf* Hitler had articulated his concept of the new Nazi order: "the establishment of a pan-German racial state from which non-Aryans were to be excluded and whose future was to be secured by the conquest of lebensraum in Eastern Europe."[14] Hitler was consistent and unrelenting about establishing his new world order even if not all "fit . . . a consistent ideological pattern but seemed outright repudiation of his ideological program."[15] Rich continues that going to war against Britain and the Scandinavians, both Aryan peoples, was hardly a case of fighting against inferior races because all or most of Britain and Scandinavia were racially superior from Hitler's racial point of view. Then his attitude toward his allies, Bulgarians, Croats, and some Serbs, certainly does not argue that all of Hitler's order was racially pure or that the world ideological scheme was perfectly in place. Totalitarianism is necessarily tactical. It can slaughter or enslave only so many of the "lesser breeds," racially or by class, at one time. The others' time will come. Totalitarianism can be successfully applied if it can employ the resources of a hegemonial state. If the industrial bureaucratic military machinery and police are efficient and able, an opportunity can be taken advantage of. Hitler's opportunity came when he occupied Eastern Europe and most of the European Russian mainland. There he captured close to five million Jews, thousands of Bolshevik apparatchiks, and Stalin's bureaucrats and military, so that his totalitarian ambitions could come to fruition. Lenin and Stalin's totalitarianism, especially that of the latter, was also a means of subjugating and eliminating peoples and races, in this case the Ukranians and the Poles, as demonstrated by the Katyn Forest massacre and the state policy of starving the Ukranians. Stalin's victory in World War II opened an opportunity for Stalinist totalitarianism in Eastern Europe, where he exported the machinery to purge and eliminate "the enemies of the people," the opposition socialists and democrats. Hitler's policy toward the Jews and the Slavs perfectly conformed to his racial theories and ambitions. As Rich says: "In my opinion such underestimation of the influence of Hitler's ideology goes so far."[16] In other words, Hitler was consistent in his war aims, even if he made certain exceptions, probably meant to last only for the duration of the war, of aligning himself with what he perceived to be inferior races. "With respect to the Jews and the Slavs, Hitler at least provided ideological guidelines for future Nazi policies."[17] His war on the USSR and against the Jews in the East was the culmination of the Nazi idea of creating a world order: the Slavic elites were to be eliminated, inferiors subjugated, and the Jews totally and indiscriminately destroyed. Occupation of the Soviet Union was left to Hitler's chief racial ideologue, Alfred Rosenberg, a German Balt himself, who was a central figure in the German military administration that ruled the central Holocaust region, Eastern Europe—Byelorussia, western Ukraine, and the Baltic states.

President Wilson did not make use of either the machinery of the state or the opportunity to impose his world order on Europe. A nonimperialist constitutional democracy, the United States does not lend its state machinery and its hegemonial power to impose its preferred world order through force. Nor did the United States have the opportunity before the Cold War to export American exceptionalism to Europe and elsewhere. But when the opportunity arrived after 1945, FDR's successors took advantage of American hegemonial power to export American democracy, mainly through economic means—the Marshall Plan, foreign aid, and the organization of an American-European military alliance, NATO—against communism. The American government did not hesitate to use covert actions to influence elite magazines and American students, as well as such propaganda agencies as Radio Free Europe and Radio Liberty. An essential difference separated the U.S. Wilsonian efforts to persuade the world of the benevolence of the American world order and those of the Nazis and communists. The latter used military and police agencies to enforce their world order and propaganda, whereas it was abhorrent behavior for an American constitutional democracy to use its mighty military machine to impose its values and order on the rest of the world.

Hitler's goals for Germany and the new world order would be fulfilled and carried out by the most virulently ideological tools of the Nazis, the SS and Waffen SS, led by another racial theorist and practitioner, Heinrich Himmler. Himmler set out to fulfill the Germanization program by transferring the population of Germans who lived in Slav lands. In addition to the Germanization program, the Final Solution to the Jewish question was fulfilled once Eastern Europe was occupied by Himmler's SS and was done with both tacit and open German Wehrmacht support. Himmler, the crank, the phantasmagoric racist, made Slavic areas the central slaughterhouse for fulfilling the German master race ideal of *lebensraum*. The emphasis on German and non-German administration in the occupied East was based on Hitler and Himmler's idea that only the Germans could rule the East. Although they had ample opportunities to gain support of Balts, Ukrainians, and other anti-Russian and anti-Stalin peoples, neither Hitler, Himmler, nor Rosenberg allowed non-Aryans and Slavs, however anticommunist and anti-Semitic, to gain senior positions in the German administration of the East. The new world order had to be Wagnerian phantasmagoria, subjugating useful and collaborating non-Aryans on an opportunistic basis. The policy of Aryanization was merciless, the bloodiest and most "logical" of all of Hitler's occupation policies. There is no comparison between Hitler's attitude toward Dutch and Norwegian defiance, Belgians under the occupation, or even the French collaborators, and his attitude toward the peoples of the East. Once again, this was related to his concept of a world order. Hitler exhibited no ambivalence about the role of the Slavs in the new world order as he did toward Germanic Nordic people like Norwegians, Danes, and even the Dutch; they would be subservient to the Germanic order. Jews in Slavic lands were to be annihilated or enslaved, turned into beasts, or exterminated. They could not play even a minor role in the administration of the new Germanic order that Hitler established in the East. Political pacification meant the ethnic cleansing of the racial opponents—Himmler's SS's major task in the East. Germanization was the equivalent of a Nazi new world order, and Hitler and Himmler mobilized and dedicated considerable resources in manpower and material to fulfill this racial fever.

Of course, the elimination of the Jews played a special role. German Jews, Polish Jews, Greek Jews, and any other Jews were all to be exterminated. Hitler and Himmler discriminated between types of Slavs, all being inferior and subjugated but some being better than others—Croats better than Serbs, Ukrainians than Russians—and they were treated according to this classification. Hitler was seriously committed to a racial war. This was the purpose of his invasion of the Soviet Union, not just passionate and irrational anticommunism. At the center was a rational, racial theory that provided the framework for his action. The bipartite or tripartite Russian-Bolshevik or Russian-Jewish-Bolshevik enemy became one. The concept of *Judeobolshevismus*, the combination of ideology and race, was not unusual. From Hitler's point of view, Bolshevism was a Jewish doctrine that polluted the Slavic people, especially Russia, both racially and ideologically. This is a most significant aspect of Hitler's racial order that he took very seriously and that enabled him to combine all of his passions in one.

Once the lands of "inferior" races were occupied, Hitler had to resort to the use of racial police. This was the special arena of Hitler's chief policeman, Heinrich Himmler, and his SS, the blackshirts who served as the praetorian guard of the new racial order, as well as its enforcers and executors. This was the group that was invested with the duty of carrying out the elimination of the Jews and the enslavement of the Slavs. Himmler and his coterie of ideologues believed that they were the elite of the racial state, its protector and policeman. Once the SS had helped Hitler eliminate political opposition, the creation of the new racial world order gave it a newfound sense of mission.

The SS was not only the task force of Nazism, it even had an international brigade attached to the regular army in the form of the Waffen SS. It was these SS troops who murdered in the trail of the armies, who set up the murder camps, and whose members commanded the death camps. They had begun their mission in Germany in 1936, building, running, and policing concentration camps. Now, they became the masters of the faith in the occupied territories of Europe, in fierce competition with the army. This task was not a function of the Nazi Party. The party as a mass movement was not significant in Hitler's occupation policy. The SS became a state within a state, as Hitler promoted his own instrument of domination, which had the effect of actually marginalizing the Nazi Party. The Nazi government and the rising SS would become the dominant powers in Hitler's Germany and the architects and practitioners of the new racial order.

Under Himmler, the SS became "the real and essential instrument of the Fuhrer's authority."[18] It would fulfill Hitler's major goals before the establishment of a new order: the destruction of the Jews and the Bolsheviks and the enslavement of Eastern Europe. The first steps toward that goal had been taken as far back as 1934 with the passing of the Nuremberg laws, which would eventually culminate in the death camps in occupied Poland and Russia. The road to the Final Solution was paved with bad intentions all along the way. At the Nazi Party Conference of 1938, Hermann Göring declared, "Should the German Reich come into conflict at any time in the foreseeable future with a foreign power, the first thing we Germans would obviously think of would be our final reckoning with the Jews."[19] The Final Solution in the occupied East was carried out by the planning and organization of the death camps and the capture and rounding up of the victims by the SS Einsatzgruppen. The next victims would be the Bolshevik apparatchiks and officers who would be assassinated or enslaved.

After the occupation of the Soviet Union, Hitler's new order would have achieved the Aryanization of the East, and the concept of race and space would be linked. The Nazi new order aims in the war were documented in the Commisar-Befehl, in which Minister of Propaganda Joseph Goebbels wrote in April 1940:

> We are now engaged in a revolution in Europe, exactly like that which we have carried through on a smaller scale in Germany. The only difference is in dimension. The principles, experiences and methods of those days are still valid today and are also effective between nations. . . . In the past, when we were asked how we expected to solve this or that problem, we always replied that we did not yet know. Of course, we had our plans, but we did not expose them to public criticism. Today if people ask us how we are going to create the new Europe, we have to reply that we do not know. Of course we have our ideas on the subject, but to publicize them would immediately create enemies and strengthen the opposition. As soon as we have gained control, everyone will see—and we, too, shall see—how we intend to use it . . . today we talk about "vital living space." Anyone can make of that what he likes. We shall know well enough what to do when the time is ripe. . . . So far we have succeeded in keeping the enemy in the dark about Germany's (that is to say, National Socialism's) real aims just as we managed to keep our political opponents before 1932 from guessing our ultimate intentions and from realizing that our apparent loyalty to legalistic conceptions was simply a smokescreen.[20]

Hitler would set up "Free Republics" after the destruction of Bolshevism "to administer and exploit the USSR as vital living space." In Himmler's words, Germany "need[s] Russia as slave labour for our civilization."[21] The territories of exiled Slavs would be resettled by German minorities. Himmler wrote about the "creation of a Pan-Europe"—Hitler's vision of a traditional European state system—when sovereign nations and legal systems would be replaced by a Pan-German European extended Reich.[22] It would be a Pan-Europe dominated by Germany, which would become a world power to "show a bold front" to the United States.[23]

To accomplish this goal, there would be shootings of commissars and mass executions of Soviet prisoners of war, all performed by SS Sonderkommando. The Wehrmacht would win the war in the East, but because its officer corps was increasingly distrusted by Hitler, it would be left to the Waffen SS to carry out the most brutal and murderous acts leading to the creation of the new Nazi world order. These efforts were legitimized by a group of professors and specialists in history, language, anthropology, and geography, some of them with dubious qualifications, known as *Ostforschung*. "We need Raum but no Polish lice in our future," wrote Professor Otto Riche, a Leipzig university professor who was an expert on racial matters, especially Slav minorities.[24] In 1940, he was a Nazi adviser to the SS in the East and wrote to one of his colleagues: "I am absolutely of the opinion that the racial-scientific side is determinative to the solution of all of these questions since we do not want to build a German people in the East in the future that would only be a linguistically Germanized, racial mishmash with strong Asiatic elements, and Polish in character. That would be no German *Volk*, nor a corner stone for a German future. . . . Since I also know the anthropological conditions in Poland and know what is racially and hereditarily useful in this people and what at all events is to be driven out of the German settlement area, I believe I have gathered together in the course of many years several ideas which should now be used for the general good and for our future."[25]

Hitler's plan to use the SS as "an anti-Bolshevistic combat organization" became a reality in the East. Hitler's racial utopia appeared to be imminent, accompanied by ethnic cleansing, murder, and destruction. Race and imperialism were the ideological creed of the Waffen SS rank and file as well as of its officers. *Lebensraum* was Himmler's vision of the world empire and order. "After the greater German Reich will come the Germanic Reich, as far as the Urals and perhaps then also the Gothic-Franconian-Carolingian Reich."[26]

Hitler's new world order was at its zenith in 1941. He had conquered most of Western, Central, and Eastern Europe and subjugated to protectorate status Croatia, Slovakia, and the

Balkan nations. With his racial shock troops and Waffen SS leading the way, he set about to annihilate some six million Jews, along with millions of Ukranians, Poles, Russians, and Gypsies. The racial utopia was being fulfilled in Slav lands, employing the best German army assembled since the days of Bismarck. Hitler had different occupation policies in Denmark, Norway, and Hungary, which he occupied for their strategic resources. He occupied the Slavic lands for the fulfillment of racial annihilation. Hitler hated the French, but he reluctantly collaborated with Vichy. He failed to take advantage of the traditional and deep hatred the nations of Ukraine and Belorus held for Stalin and Russia. Very likely he could have enlisted these nations and turned them on Russia, dismantled the USSR, and forced Stalin to retreat to the Urals, thereby winning the war in the East. Instead, Hitler treated the Soviet nationalities the same as the Jews and Russian Slavs and Bolsheviks, that is, his forces brutalized and set about exterminating them. Here, he was ruled by his overriding racial vision, which was the chief purpose of the war. Hitler's racial concept of world order led him to and over the abyss.

For a time, the East became a fiefdom for Himmler and the SS. It was a short-lived but very real example of what Hitler's and Himmler's new world order might have looked like had it succeeded. The war itself ended the vision, aptly and primarily at the hands of Stalin's Red Army, but not before millions of people had suffered and died. The war brought to an end the utopia that had its most vivid reality in the minds and imaginations of Hitler and Himmler.[27]

Between them, Hitler and Stalin destroyed the Wilsonian-Versailles international order. No one can ever accuse Adolf Hitler of being an internationalist, seeking world peace. He was a ruthless racist seeking German-Nazi hegemony over Europe and the world. Hitler's racial utopia was as far detached from reality as was Lenin's classless society. Both Hitler and Lenin's heir Stalin meant to fulfill their world order through force and conquest, an approach that clearly separates them from Wilson's American-dominated, pacifistic world order. Yet world order was their purpose, and each was guided by his own vision of the world and the place of his nation in it.

The Nazi-Soviet pact of August 1939, known as the Devils' Pact, was forged between the heads of two totalitarian world orders, both antagonistic to the Wilsonian order and seeking its destruction. The collusion between these two totalitarian world orders in the end did not represent a joint conspiracy, as it began. Stalin and Hitler had different agendas to pursue, which converged by 1939. This was either misperceived or not effectively challenged by the narrow-minded post-Versailles European statesmen and diplomats, particularly the French, who, in their zeal and fear of a resurgent Germany and their animosity toward communism, isolated the two great land powers of Europe, Germany and Russia (now the USSR).[28]

The French considered the League of Nations, as well as the small, newly formed Eastern European states, instruments of security against Germany. This, combined with French revanchism, represented in their ruthless reparation policy, may be well understood because France's World War I losses were the greatest of all the participants. The concept of *Sécurité* meant formation of small alliances, with Czechoslovakia, Romania, and Poland, to prevent the reemergence of Germany. Neither worked. The reparation policy was counterproductive, as the economist John Maynard Keynes pointed out in 1919, and the small alliances, involving mostly authoritarian radical nationalist states, which, according to Rothschild, had only anti-Semitism in common, were of little use to the French. The isolation of the USSR had the same effect in the end on the demise of Versailles. Instead of establishing a new world order of peace, stability, security, and democracy, all of the successor states to the Austro-Hungarian, Ottoman, Russian, and German empires, with the exception of Czechoslovakia, were autocratic or military regimes, characterized by radical ethnicism and fervent anti-Semitism. The absence of America in the League and its failure to recognize the Soviet Union until 1933 also contributed to the demise of Wilsonianism and Versailles. As Germany recovered and the USSR experienced the pains of Stalin's collectivization and purges, the Nazi challenge became more serious and effective. Weimar's Gustav Stresemann, a European statesman who could be dealt with, died in 1929. Germany was now pursuing a new world order that sought no compromise short of racial supremacy in Europe. The British Conservative government was impotent: it was more anti-Soviet than anti-Nazi. If the Soviet "menace" was perceived in the 1920s and early 1930s, once Hitler came to power it was perceived as even more ominous. Chamberlain appeased Hitler, not Stalin.

The fact that the United States was absent from the international system, the fact that Wilson's plan for world order collapsed and was defeated by the U.S. Senate, the fact that the British and French did not seek to coordinate a more reasonable policy toward Germany, and the fact that Stalin had his own agenda (moving west) demonstrated not only the absence of a world order but also the absence of the United States as the only party willing to take the responsibility for creating one. The absence of a Wilsonian concept of international order left the two totalitarian powers to collude. The French obsession with security and their reinforcement of Versailles did not augur well for the future of European order. The demilitarization of the Rhine, and above all the occupation of the Ruhr, left the Weimar Republic in a quandary. Only under the wise statesmanship of Gustav Stresemann, the Weimar foreign minister, who persuaded both the French and the British that the Weimar Republic sought a settlement of the German question within Europe, was short-term stability achieved. The failure to understand the importance of Germany for Europe or to understand and realize the potential of Soviet expansionism, that Stalin's so-called policy of "socialism in one country" was a cover-up for an international revolutionary movement represented by the Comintern, Stalin's surrogate world order, led to disaster.

Between 1929 and 1931, a glimpse of hope emerged in the post-Locarno disarmament conferences. But disarmament was interpreted as a policy related to French security and not to the European world order. The admission of Germany to the League was important but not sufficient. Once again, the world was characterized by what Wilson said it should not be: a mania for pacts, alliances, military buildup, authoritarian governments, fascism, Nazism, anti-Semitism, and ethnocentrism, and was not guided by empires of the past, which were the real villains to Wilson. The glaring absence of an American international order was apparent, and the European powers, especially France, could not get their act together. Seeking a policy that was more vital to its defense than to the stability of Europe was represented to be the tragedy of the absence of an American order. Locarno and the Eastern alliances were a poor option for security, as Stalin and Hitler came closer together. The spirit of Rapallo would win over the spirit of Locarno.

CHAPTER 5

Resurrection of Wilsonianism
FDR

By 1940–41, Britain was fighting for its life, and a Nazi order had been established in Europe. The fear now was that an occupied Western Europe, minus Spain, Portugal, and Switzerland, presented a threat to American interests. This fear brought a turnabout in President Franklin D. Roosevelt's policy toward intervention, causing him to challenge the isolationists. Even if the United States was not ready for war, and the president said the United States would provide "aid short of war," the country was inching in that direction. The problem facing the president was how to educate American public opinion and persuade an isolationist Congress that intervention might become necessary.

Between August 9 and 12, 1941, Roosevelt and Churchill met aboard a ship anchored in Placentia Bay. The result of this meeting was the Atlantic Charter. It was "a vague and general statement about Anglo-American war aims, it was designed for public consumption, and to ward off the attacks of American anti-interventionists."[1] The Atlantic Charter was not a Wilsonian charter, but it was moored on Wilsonian principles. The president was not ready for more than limited participation in the European war, certainly not until American public opinion would legitimize such a policy. Thus cooperation with Britain was all the Atlantic Charter was about.

Yet the seeds of neo-Wilsonianism had been planted. After all, the charter stipulated collective security, end of colonialism, open foreign policy, end of aggression, and peaceful settlement of disputes. What are these, if not Wilsonian principles? Thus the Atlantic Charter could be said to be the first step toward a reemergent Wilsonianism. In fact, the charter was the first document that indicated that the United States had abandoned its isolation in World War II and was ready to participate in a new postwar structure for peace.[2] Even if the Atlantic Charter was not "congenial" to Roosevelt, it nevertheless was a start.[3] Even if Roosevelt's understanding of foreign policy was not terribly sophisticated, he was an internationalist. As Theodore Wilson noted, "There was to be much of Wilsonian idealism in the Atlantic Charter."[4]

In what sense was the Atlantic Charter a Wilsonian instrument? First, it called for no territorial aggrandizement and for respect for sovereignty of states. Second, it called for the right of people to choose their governments. Third, it called for bringing about a fair and equitable distribution of essential produce, not only within individual nations' territorial jurisdiction but between the nations of the world—that is, free trade. Fourth, it called for the creation of an effective international organization for peace.[5] In other words, it involved the end of colonialism, or imperialism in any form, and the substitution of the new order for the old one. Disarmament was also intended to end colonialism, not a favorite topic with Churchill. But the most substantial Wilsonian article in the Atlantic Charter was trade liberalization, an essential postwar policy. Even if at this stage the president was not ready to support the revival of a world organization; he was still thinking of "a new assembly of the League." Only after the United States entered the war in 1941 was the planning for the international order intensified and the principle of collective security turned back to the Council of Nations, especially championed by the American president.[6]

The president was dedicated to collective security, to a neo-Wilsonian international system to be called the United Nations. Stalin, however, in the old nineteenth-century balance-of-power tradition, saw the future of international politics and Europe in a totally different perspective than the president. Their worldviews were asymmetrical and in the end irreconcilable. Some diplomatic historians have argued that Roosevelt was actually dedicated to a sphere-of-influence international system. To collaborate with Stalin, the policy of the marginalization of Europe was designed to promote peace and U.S. interests. To promote peace and U.S. interests, Elena Aga-Rossi suggests, "As early as 1942 Roosevelt held the following positions: 1) collaboration with the USSR was the most important American objective for maintaining the post-war peace and promoting US interests; 2) collaboration with the USSR was possible as long as Soviet requests and 'legitimate interests' in Europe and in Asia were satisfied; 3) the division of Europe into spheres of influence between Britain and the Soviet Union was not only inevitable, but desirable."[7] Thus revisionist historians have designed a policy for the president that he never articulated or clearly explained to friend or rival, never mentioned either in speeches or in press conferences, and never discussed at length with his allies Churchill and especially Stalin. All these assumptions of "spheres of influence," which have been called elsewhere "spheres of responsibility,"[8] are unconvincing. In a democracy, foreign policy is not secret. Congress and the American people knew that FDR was dedicated to collective security. Extensive research in the Soviet archives has not produced any reference in Stalin's and his advisers' writings that any understanding regarding spheres of influence was actually received as the president's policy by Stalin, V. M. Molotov, or Stalin's U.S. ambassadors. The spheres-of-influence policy, peddled by some revisionist historians, is half-tea, half-coffee realpolitik. The leading proponent of this notion is Lloyd C. Gardner, who writes that FDR "went beyond Churchill in making concessions, these were somehow different but in terms of permanence and implication."[9] The revisionists argue that the president at Yalta sought to bring an end to the "beautiful ideas,"[10] meaning that the president supposedly abandoned his commitment to collective security.

To accommodate both Churchill and Stalin, the president went back to his opaque idea that has never developed intellectually or as a policy which is known as the Four Policemen concept.

Warren Kimball demonstrates the president's inconsistency and lack of profound thinking and commitments in foreign policy when, in Teheran, "FDR put it clearly to the Soviet leader—we need to talk about 'a great many other matters pertaining to the future of the world.'"[11] "When Stalin said they could discuss whatever they wished, Roosevelt launched into a description of the postwar international organization he envisaged. Stalin cut directly to the dilemma—would this body (an executive committee composed of the Big Four plus six other states) 'make decisions binding on the world?' Roosevelt then spoke of the Four Policemen who would deal with emergency threats to the peace."[12] Kimball claims that "Roosevelt's image of impulsiveness usually masked a consistent pattern."[13] But if there is a consistent pattern to be discerned in Roosevelt's foreign policy, it is the *opposite* of patient design or careful planning. Kimball further argued that "Roosevelt had a conscious, structured foreign policy, even if there was an enormous gap between concept and implementation." I would argue that the foreign policy FDR pursued—the one he "implemented"—lacked a coherent and viable conceptual pattern.

The revisionist argument is based on an unrealistic, unfounded understanding of the Soviet system and Stalin. There is yet no iota of proof that Roosevelt had any understanding whatsoever, or interest, or perception, or depth, of the Soviet system or believed that the Soviet Union would become a "normal" state. Kimball states that President Roosevelt "expected Stalin's cooperation for the postwar European order" and believed that the Soviet Union "would abandon Marxism-Leninism and expansionism in favor of collaboration and European stability" because "Roosevelt always had tended to underestimate Soviet ideology, dismissing it as something of the past."[14] This neorevisionist interpretation demonstrates Roosevelt to be a more systematically insubstantial international dreamer than he actually appeared to be, by emphasizing the policy of coming to terms with Stalin in the hopes that the USSR would become normal (an outlandish view because there was no chance in the world that Stalin's USSR would turn normal).[15]

The president must be seen from the vantage point of international political theory as neither a realist nor an idealist. He preferred to be considered an idealist, but actually he was a blend between Woodrow Wilson and Teddy Roosevelt, and he was not profoundly committed to any international theory. We cannot help but reach the conclusion that he had no profound understanding of international politics, that he was a Johnny-come-lately to it in World War II, and that his writings and speeches in foreign policy began in 1937 and are statements of dubious profundity.[16] The fact is that the marginalization of Europe, which already meant the end of the European great power system, was at best an uninformed, profoundly ignorant understanding of European politics and diplomacy. The president's suggestion that breaking down Yugoslavia and Czechoslovakia would bring an end to ethnic strife as part of the process of creating stability in a marginalized Europe demonstrates fifty years later the danger this policy represented. Aga-Rossi writes, "Roosevelt had no sympathy for smaller European countries such as Finland or even Poland. He did not believe that democratic institutions could be established in Eastern Europe."[17] I would argue that leaving the fate of Eastern Europe to Stalin was not so much a betrayal as a misguided policy: surrendering to Stalin what was not *his*, in the belief that it would become "ours."

Certainly Roosevelt believed that he could not create a new international order or an effective United Nations organization without Stalin. But FDR's collective security strategy, moored in a world organization, very soon collapsed and ended in the Cold War because of his indifference to and ignorance of Stalin's traditionally Russian strategy, a strategy anchored in the old European balance-of-power international political order.[18] All Roosevelt wanted was to keep the United States out of European power politics and to delegate authority instead to a surrogate international order—the United Nations. FDR supposedly never resolved in his own mind whether he was more committed to ridding Europe of its old ills of imperialism than to maintaining collective security. At least collective security would have meant an end to the balance of power, which was, in FDR's view, the conceptual tool of Old World European imperialists. Collective security was FDR's global New Deal, wherein Stalin's Russia—not old Britain and France—became the United States's senior partner.

The president's view of Poland as a "small detail" demonstrates his lack of appreciation for Stalin's grand design. It cannot be denied that the issue of Poland was a key in the Yalta agenda. We cannot escape the fact that at the second most important summit (Roosevelt's last), the issue of Poland loomed large. It loomed large precisely because it related to Stalin's strategy. Poland was certainly irrelevant to the president, as some of us have demonstrated, but not to Stalin. The question is not who lost Poland but, what did Poland represent? The Polish issue clearly represented Stalin's postwar territorial aspirations, strategies, and design. If it was not of great significance to the president, in his unrelenting effort to accept Stalin's geographic and territorial aspirations as a price paid for the establishment of the United Nations (possibly President Roosevelt's most important issue at Yalta), then the marginalization of European spheres-of-influence theory loses its raison d'être. The issue of Poland once again pitted the two strategists against each other: the new "league" and collective security versus Old World balance of power. Even to those who argue that the president was dedicated to some sort of spheres of influence, the Polish issue represents *Stalin's* concern for his sphere without reciprocity to the president, except for an indifferent accommodation with FDR's new league idea. The president's real betrayal was on the issue of elections to the Polish government (i.e., betrayal of promises he made to millions of American-Polish voters at home). He did not lose or win Poland. The issue of Poland must be dealt with in terms of the conflicting strategies of Roosevelt and Stalin. The issue is not, as some believe, that "Roosevelt lost Europe at Yalta because of his naivete about Stalin's intentions" or that "the division of Europe was inevitable after the Yalta conference since Soviet troops had already occupied the disputed territories."[19] The Stalin-FDR relationship concerning the future of Europe was linked to the president's illusions of collaboration with a normal USSR after the war. It was not naive but foolish.[20]

The peace FDR sought and the strategy he proposed for Europe (if it had been implemented) would have been an even greater disaster than merely coming to terms with Stalin. The point once more is that there was no way to come to terms with Stalin, whose strategy and purposes for the future of peace in Europe were totally divergent from the president's. What is tragic about the president's failure as a diplomat is that he not only ignored Stalin's purposes but also failed to understand Stalin's strategy, the Soviet system; above all, Roosevelt had a monumental ignorance of the history and international relations of Europe. The price for appeasing Stalin was the marginalization of Europe, which would have had disastrous effects if it had been fulfilled. Just imagine Europe with a shrunken Britain, a hardly existent France, a divided Germany, dominated by a European hegemon, Russia, led by the *vozhd*, Stalin.

The president wanted to establish a system based on open markets, free enterprise, and neo-Wilsonian international collective security. The president was not naive. On the contrary, he was one of the most Machiavellian of American politicians; but he did not demonstrate this trait in international politics. One could be charitable and say that he meant well. But the opposite was true: he was arrogant in believing he could sway Stalin to think his way.

The president never made himself clear (orally or on paper) at length or consistently about his postwar strategy. Roosevelt had no doctrine or strategy for the postwar period. He was an improviser, as he was in implementing the New Deal, moving inconsistently from one project to another. Because of his political acumen and sensitivity, he depended more on his intuition than on an established strategic conception. He was a man of enormous intuition and equally undisciplined. He conducted the war on the basis of his intuition and allowed his generals to devise a military strategy. We can debate this question until the end of time. If the president indeed had a spheres-of-influence policy in mind, as the neorevisionists claim, we would have been less charitable about him than we are toward his more sensible neo-Wilsonian collective security concept. FDR, at heart a Wilsonian determinist, set out to establish and institutionalize a collective security system for the postwar international order. Preparations were already being made when FDR and Churchill signed the Atlantic Charter, when a reluctant Churchill did everything within his power to make sure that the United States would become involved in the war. With the United States not yet in the war as a belligerent, FDR and Churchill signed a general Anglo-American statement on war aims, which would become the foundation for a new collective security system for the new postwar order. Secretary of State Cordell Hull, a bona fide Wilsonian, established a special division within the State Department dealing solely with the issue of postwar peace.

By 1944, a draft charter for what would become the United Nations had been devised. FDR set the basic format, which would eventually evolve into the five-member Security Council, a concept of European great powers with a veto, linking an executive body (the Security Council) to a General Assembly made up of the nations of the world. This was not going to be another League of Nations because the United States would play a crucial participatory role, as would the USSR. Oddly, Stalin was at first very reluctant and dismissive about the idea of a postwar coalition, but at Yalta, he agreed to a Soviet role, buttressed by veto power, in the United Nations. Stalin and Churchill were classic balance-of-power imperialists, whatever their ideological inclinations, and both were lukewarm about the United Nations.

But in 1945, American military, atomic, economic, and political power was overwhelmingly pervasive and persuasive. Churchill was aware that Great Britain was becoming a second-rate power, even though intellectually and emotionally he never fully accepted that unpleasant reality. The United Nations was FDR Wilsonianism with a vengeance.

This time, the prosletyzers and champions of collective security would be in charge, guiding an international organization that would be both potent and aggressive, with the United States, the only real superpower in the world, at its center. That hope did not last very long. The emerging Cold War, springing from Stalin's betrayals at Yalta, thinned the enthusiasm for collective security, turning the United Nations into a Cold War battleground. The epitome of this occurred in 1950, when North Korea, supported by Stalin, invaded South Korea, and the United States could still exploit the United Nations for its own purposes.

The actions of Presidents Wilson, Roosevelt, Truman, and their successors (with the exception of Carter) represented a mixture of moralism and realism, liberalism and realpolitik. And one would be extremely naive to propose that any American president in the twentieth century (including Roosevelt) was either one or the other. The case must rest on whether Roosevelt's policy was, as I argue, more consistently dedicated to collective security, or the opposing view, that he was dedicated to spheres of influence; neither policy moved Stalin an iota from his strategy, brought any benefits to American interests, or preserved the peace.

Roosevelt's war goals were crusading in nature, to fight a holy war to defeat the totalitarian Axis nations, in particular the evils of Nazism and fascism. In this, he and the alliance he forged and sometimes led succeeded. *But his vision for a postwar world was neo-Wilsonian, totally at odds with reality.* He would help create a new international order, presided over in an equal partnership by the two emerging superpowers, the United States and the USSR, and buttressed by the newly created world organization, the United Nations.

FDR's wartime diplomacy, geared to his vision of the postwar world, was fueled by what could almost be called a desperate desire to fulfill the dream that the Soviets would be America's postwar partner. This required an amazing ignorance, a willingness to ignore past and present facts, and a complete misunderstanding of the Soviet system and of Stalin. FDR was right that the United States and the Soviet Union would be the postwar superpowers, but he was absolutely and disastrously wrong about the nature of their future relationship. According to George Kennan, "The Russian involvement in this struggle is not the result of any concern for the principles underlying the Allied cause . . . Russia has tried unsuccessfully to purchase security by compromising with Germany and by encouraging the direction of the German war effort toward the west. . . . It has thus no claim on Western sympathies; and there is no reason apparent to me why its present plight should not be viewed realistically at home as that of one who has played a lone hand in a dangerous game and must now alone take the moral consequences. Such a view would not preclude the extension of material aid wherever called for by our own self-interest. It would, however, preclude anything which might identify us politically or ideologically with the Russian war effort."[21]

FDR's diplomacy and postwar vision were wrong from the outset, based on a unworkable premise that poisoned any number of political-military decisions throughout the war. FDR was wrong because he never understood or wanted to understand; he never inquired into the nature and structure of the Soviet political system, as did, for instance, George Kennan, the brilliant young State Department officer and Soviet specialist who lost all of his illusions about the nature of Soviet conduct early in the game.

If one judges success by achieving stated war aims, then FDR gained direct military triumph, but he saw all the war's ideal objectives buried in abject failures, and FDR had only himself to blame for his failure. For the most part, he chose advisers who would tell him what he wanted to hear. Those with bad news, warnings, or forebodings and misgivings about the Soviets were cut off from the president or were ignored. Speaking of FDR's deficiencies and the "unreal assumptions on Roosevelt's part," Kennan believed these deficiencies were shared by his civilian and military advisers. "Altogether, these efforts, not only by FDR but by others on the American side as well, to achieve a special relationship to Stalin, even at the cost of demeaning the prestige and authority of the President's own Western allies, and Churchill in particular, stand as one of the saddest manifestations of the almost childish failure on FDR's part to understand the personality of Stalin himself and the nature of his regime."[22] Speaking especially of the military advisers, Kennan claims "it is perhaps not too much to say that senior American commanders who came into contact with their Soviet opposite numbers in the course of our wartime association found their personal relations with their senior opposite numbers in the Soviet armed forces to be less troubled than their comparable relations with their British counterparts. Of particular importance were of course the relations between Gen. Dwight Eisenhower and his soviet counterpart Marshal G. K. Zhukov." Kennan continues, stating that "senior American commanders continued to the very end of the war in Europe to be strongly affected by their admiration for the dimensions and power of the Soviet ground-force effort in Europe and by the fear that it might be terminated by some sort of a separate Soviet peace with Hitler if political differences between the Soviet leadership and the Western Allies came to be aired before the hostilities were over."[23] But this was not true of all American officers. Those officers "who were sent to the Soviet Union were required to deal with the Soviet military and civilian bureaucracies on the spot gained quite different and far less reassuring impressions of the Soviet military establishment than those then current among their superiors in Washington."[24] In Kennan's view, civilian and military advisers "departed from what we would have considered the requirements of strict realism."[25]

FDR's behavior and attitudes at Teheran and Yalta, and the attitudes of his surrogate diplomats (Harry Hopkins and Averill Harriman) that reflected his, led to his diplomatic failure. The world he envisioned and so desperately wanted to create never materialized and, more important, never had a chance of materializing because it rested on a false premise, buttressed by willful ignorance. FDR did not have a glimmer that the pursuit of his vision, and the concessions he made to it, would result, not in a partnership with Stalin and the USSR, but rather in its opposite, in the onset of the Cold War that would last almost half a century. The Yalta Conference, according to Kennan, "was the last of the summit meetings still outwardly dominated, at least on the American side, by the cultivation of this essentially fictitious and misleading scenario."[26]

Since the president was his own diplomat, secretary of state, and national security chief, he alone bears full and direct responsibility for America's diplomatic failure in World War II. The great war leader failed to win the peace.

Franklin Roosevelt's political grandeur in the twentieth century stands almost purely on the basis of his leadership, first during the Great Depression and later, and more important, during World War II. There is no question that FDR was a great war leader, not in substance, detail, or strategy, but by the sheer force of his personality and magnetism. He was a great generalist, not a great general, and he could describe, mobilize, and lead the American war effort with dramatic and rhetorical power. His place in history is secure; he mobilized America to a war against Nazism.

His virtues—the ability to lead with passion, to be unencumbered by and indeed to ignore detail, his belief in his own vision, and his ability to project supreme optimism—made him a great leader. But those qualities were also flaws that produced an unreasoning blindness and an unwillingness to deal with reality in his pursuit of not clearly defined Wilsonian goals.

His record, his personality, and his popularity made him the perfect war president. He was the commander in chief in deed and perception. He was "the administration," which made his job of leading the nation through the war much easier. Getting into the war was another matter, and Pearl Harbor made that hotly debated issue a moot one. With the Japanese attack, FDR no longer needed to seek congressional support—there was no question that he would get it.

Before that, Roosevelt had wrestled with his own doubt and, more difficult, with the strong isolationist forces in Congress. He had hedged before, first by inclination, then by political necessity, at becoming a direct belligerent, but there was no question where his sympathies lay. Slowly, and with considerable political maneuvering, he managed to move Congress and public opinion toward the idea that the question was no longer whether the country would enter the war, but when.

Most of his rivals found it difficult to understand him, to find some consistent theme that would enable them to anticipate future action. Hitler was a Eurocentrist who was profoundly ignorant of the United States, and he misinterpreted Roosevelt's gentlemanly posture and easygoing style as signs of a lack of hardness and fiber.

FDR was not a military strategist, but he never pretended to be one. In this, he differed markedly from Churchill, Hitler, and Stalin, each of whom embodied and symbolized the great war strategist for his country. Hitler directly guided and interfered with every detail, following his vaunted intuition, overriding his generals, proclaiming his military genius in the war with the USSR with disastrous results. Stalin, too, had total control over his country's military operations. Even Churchill liked to think of himself as a brilliant strategist, and he drove his generals to fits of distraction with his meddling.

FDR was wise enough to leave the actual running of the war largely to his generals and military advisers, especially Generals George C. Marshall and Eisenhower. He trusted them completely and relied heavily on Marshall. The generals had few if any political axes to grind. They were able, competent, sometimes brilliant, and, more important, they understood the president's distaste for detail, sparing him the complex operational plans of their campaigns.

The qualities that made him a great war leader had nothing to do with military thinking; rather it was his determination, his personality, his authoritarian behavior, and his projection of absolute confidence that made him, along with Churchill and Stalin, a great war leader.

But just as FDR was a great war leader, so he was also a great failure as a diplomat. He helped win the war, but he lost the peace. This is not a resurrection of the old warhorse charge that Roosevelt was duped by the communists. Rather, my argument is that he was deceived by his own vision. This was a tragic failure, especially for a president who had led and conducted his country in its greatest foreign war.

CHAPTER 6

Balance of Power, Balance of Terror, and the Cold War

It has been argued that after World War II a balance-of-power international order was created. As I have explained, contrary to FDR's hopes, the collective security concept did not take off, as the experience of the United Nations demonstrates; in fact, the idea of collective security was defeated as soon as World War II came to an end. A bipolar, eventually superpower, rivalry took place with bandwagons and satellites around each hegemonial power. Bipolarity was the essence of the international system after the war. It was also part of a mighty ideological struggle. The American ideology of containment and the Stalinist ideology of the march of international communism were more than dressings over the preponderance of military and political power manifested throughout the fifty years of the Cold War.

The Cold War, as I shall explain, is still a hot debate among historians and political scientists, and more so after 1989, when it was officially over. Was it a traditional balance-of-power relationship? Was it an ideological, theological rivalry? Was it a combination of the two? Going along with Paul Schroeder's concept of the balance and a theory of international relations which is independent of the system itself, I would argue that the balance of power after 1945 represented a bipolar rivalry between two major industrial, military, and political powers that was considerably different than the balance of power in nineteenth century Europe in the sense that the post-1945 system was also ideological.

It has been argued that the post–Congress of Vienna balances of power were an effort on the part of conservative, monarchical regimes in Europe to suppress the revolution, that the French Revolution upset the international system, and the balance-of-power efforts were undertaken to quell it. Whatever the purposes were, however, in the end it was a traditional balance of power, unencumbered by ideology, theology, or political philosophy.

The Cold War, in contrast, in which ideology was a significant part of power politics, helping to shape the bipolar rivalry between the Soviet Union and the United States, went beyond the traditional balance-of-power objectives of creating stability and order. Ideological zeal was apparent on both sides, as witnessed by the Soviet effort to "save" the colonial world and Sovietize it in the name of progress (which was a mask for Soviet imperialist ambitions) and the American clandestine activities and interventions in Europe that enhanced Christian democracy in Germany, Italy, and France and American intervention in the Middle East with the support of so-called anticommunist "new" middle classes, the praetorians of the Nasserite and Ba'athist movements. The Americans, especially in Latin America, were highly interventionist on behalf of authoritarian, anti-Marxist, and anticommunist military praetorians. In the name of American hegemony and ideology, the United States's clandestine instruments—the CIA and the spy network—intended to create pro-Western (i.e., pro-American) regimes. This is true not only in Latin America but also in southern Europe, where the first Papandreau government was for all intents and purposes established by the CIA. In Egypt and Syria, the Office of Strategic Services (later the CIA) played significant roles both in putting the Syrian military in power between 1952 and 1954 and in the rise of Nasser to power after 1952. Nasser's grand nationalist pronunciamento, the pamphlet *The Egyptian Revolution*, was CIA-inspired.

While Soviet interventionism was clothed with revolutionary "progressive" slogans, American intervention was shameless. The instruments of such activities—such as the CIA—knew they were supporting authoritarian, and sometimes reactionary, officers. Thus if Stalin and his successors imposed a Communist Party state police in Eastern Europe to create satellites for the Soviet Union, the regimes the United States helped to establish in the Middle East and Latin America were not "protected" by an American ideology, even though regimes were toppled and established in the name of anticommunism and pro-Americanism. This I call coerced bandwagoning.

These activities were certainly those of hegemonial powers participating in the activity called balance of power. But nevertheless, in the age of populist movements, of emergent postcolonial nationalism and ethnic groups, ideological appeals—however distorted—not only were welcomed but were successfully used by the two rival powers, except that Stalin and his successors used brute force and subservient regimes, while the United States acted out of greed and was not directly involved in the authoritarian pursuit of power of its clients.

Bipolarity in a balance-of-power system does not mean direct or indirect interventions. Wilson himself is for all intents and purposes the father of covert action, as in the case of Mexico. The nineteenth-century nation-state system was characterized by empires: the Austro-Hungarian monarchy, the British Empire, the French Empire, the Ottoman Empire, the Russian Empire, the German Empire. In other words, the aspiration for political influence, expansion, and intervention was in the name of empire. Some contiguous empires—such as the nationalities within the Austro-Hungarian or Ottoman empires—also justified expansion in the name of proximity and stability of the empire. The other empires—British and French—sought stability beyond their contiguous territory, for example, the British in India, the French in Indochina, and the British and French in their colonial conquests in Africa. Thus the struggle for power was maintained beyond Europe, in the peripheries. The monumental classic work of William F. Langer, *The Diplomacy of Imperialism*, is our most enduring source explaining the purpose and nature of this struggle.

Such was not the case in the nation-state system after 1945.

Since the Soviet Union pretended to be a universal state, even though dominated by a party state police and a Russian dictatorship, it sought imperial control under the guise of ideology. In the case of the United States, which renounced imperialistic ambitions after 1945, intervention became more difficult to explain. The regimes the United States helped to install were authoritarian, antidemocratic, oppressive, and could hardly fit either the Wilsonian concept or the American penchant for support of democratic regimes. If Stalin and his successors did not shy away from conquest of territory, postwar America rejected conquest and supported self-determination of nations and peoples. United States policy makers therefore found the situation much more complicated and hypocritically justified their actions, aware that these interventions did not support democratic forces.

The communist false utopia was used as a guise for Russian intervention and imperial domination. The Soviet Union was, until 1989, the last historical empire. The United States, rejecting the role and orientation of empire, had to find other means to sustain bipolarity and balance, by "converting" one form of Third World authoritarianism to another—again in the name of the rule of the middle class, democracy, and free trade. This did not change the essential nature of bipolarity and the balance of power, but it colored and influenced the relationship between the two rivals in ways that did not exist in the nineteenth-century balances and rivalries. It is significant that the two great powers were zealous guardians of their ultimate weapons. Both the United States and the Soviet Union were dedicated to nuclear nonproliferation and to the possession of weapons only by dominant and "responsible" powers. Third World instability did not augur well for nuclear safety. It is true that the United States was more dedicated to the regime of nonproliferation than the Soviet Union, but when it came to every system of arms control, the nuclear balance of power established between the two was to extend to the Third World nations by denying them the ability to become nuclear states. No area better represents the pure, unvarnished, ideological balance of power than that of nuclear weapons and nuclear proliferation. It is here that the two powers sustained and underlined the bipolar condition of the balance. Of course, with the end of the Cold War and the emergence of multipolarity, nuclear proliferation was quadrupled.

Thus to argue that ideology was not relevant to a bipolar rivalry is insufficient, in view of the fact that with the end of bipolarity also came the end of ideological competition, which played a key role in harnessing the proliferation of nuclear weapons only because it threatened the great powers. It is not sufficient to argue that ideology does not matter to power politics. It mattered much in the struggle between the United States and the Soviet Union. The ideological spooks have now been torn asunder and no longer help to sustain a more restrictive and controlled proliferation regime.

The Cold War was inevitable because President Roosevelt failed to resolve the major issues between himself and Stalin. He had no strategy for world order except a resurrection of some Wilsonian ideals such as collective security and a world safe for democracy and free trade. The Teheran and Yalta Conferences were designed to establish the world order after World War II. The participants in these conferences, Stalin and Roosevelt, however, failed to define and clarify a common vision of the world, simply because Joseph Stalin had no intention of establishing anything but a Leninist world order and Roosevelt had no clear vision of his own except a neo-Wilsonian order. Churchill, although a major player, was relegated to a secondary position after 1943. He fought a traditional war to preserve the British Empire, an unthreatened Europe, and a European balance of power, an East Central European confederation to separate Russia from Western Europe. A conservative nationalist, he did not have the illusions Roosevelt had.

To persuade the American people that the war against Nazism was a just cause, Roosevelt had to argue on ideological grounds, even though he did not conduct the war ideologically. Whether the public believed it or not is not relevant. The most convenient ideological underpinning was Wilson's. Roosevelt went even further in American war propaganda: he portrayed Stalin's Soviet Union as a democracy. Wilson was conscious of the uncomfortable coalition between the United States and czarist Russia before World War I, even though the United States joined the Allies after the czarist regime collapsed. Still one of the reasons why the United States did not enter the war with the Allies earlier (after 1914) was precisely the perception that the czarist regime was a tyrannical oppressive state. To form an alliance, President Wilson had to believe and hope that under a provisional government, Russia would be more progressive. There was a very strong lobby among the progressive movements, liberal democrats, the Jewish community, and the Polish Catholic Church against an alliance with czarist Russia. Had the president insisted on entering the war, he certainly would have overcome the resistance of Jewish and Catholic interests, which were still immature in their political organizational and lobbying capabilities. Nevertheless, the leading American liberal press would have pressured Wilson against such an alliance.

FDR took exactly the same position concerning Stalin, that the Soviet Union would become a normal state and eventually a liberal one. In this way, FDR made the alliance with the Soviet Union seem more palatable.

Nazism, fascism, and communism were radical, modernist mass movements. They were fighting a mission to change the world in their image. Churchill, an eighteenth-century statesman, conducted the war not only to save the British Empire but also to redress the balance of power in Europe, an old international relations strategy. Of all the actors in World War II, only Hitler and Stalin fought ideologically. Roosevelt came to the idea of collective security late in the war. Hitler fought a racial war, which was to him the raison d'être of the war. For Hitler, territorial conquest by itself was insufficient. Contrary to A. J. P. Taylor, Hitler was not a traditional European statesman. For Hitler the war in Russia was a war against the two major enemies: Jews and communists. Not in vain he called it a war against Judeo-Bolshevismus. Stalin, unquestionably a Leninist who claimed to be a Marxist, was also a traditional Russian nationalist and imperialist. He began the war to defend his country, but at the end of the war, with the Red Army marching into Berlin, Stalin clothed its conquests in idealist, ideological civilian garb. Unquestionably, his design to occupy and dominate Eastern Europe was strategic and territorial. But more than that, it was ideological. If Wilson felt comfortable in a liberal world order which he championed, Stalin felt safe in a Leninist world order. Toward the end of the war Stalin did not fight merely for ideological purposes; yet the success of the Red Army marching into Berlin rekindled the revolutionary spirit. The barbarism and brutality of the Nazi-Soviet war went far beyond traditional imperialism and traditional warfare.

These aspirations, goals, and visions were not settled, nor could they have been settled, during the war. The war was to be conducted to defeat the Axis forces. When it came to establishing a world vision, in the great conferences, FDR and Stalin did not address the issue. Yet the Leninist and Wilsonian world orders lurked underneath the surface and would emerge when the war was over. The basic division between communism and democracy was not settled in 1945, nor did the conference participants intend to settle it. Each one resolved it in a way that failed to explain their postwar intentions. The war was a watershed in the sense that when it ended, the United States and the USSR would become hegemonial powers. But it was not until the peripheral territories were settled in Eastern Europe and the Balkans that the ideological battle of the hegemons began. The year 1946 was a watershed. Stalin resolved that Leninism had won, and it was left to President Harry Truman to demonstrate that this was not so and that the United States would confront and contain Stalin's Leninist aspirations. Thus the origins of the Cold War can rightly be demonstrated in the way the war ended. It would take almost a half-century to settle the ideological divide, a division that was either ignored, postponed, overlooked, or whitewashed by President Roosevelt and left for his successor, Harry Truman.

The post–World War II U.S. Cold War policy and its articulation were created by a group of dedicated foreign service officers, joined by political figures from the New York financial and legal establishments. They certainly shared common social, intellectual, and professional characteristics—they were white Protestant graduates of elite eastern universities—and they would all play key roles in the administration of the War and Navy Departments during World War II. Secretaries James Forrestal, John McCloy, and Robert Lovett, as well as Paul Nitze and Averill Harriman (the president's personal envoy to Churchill and Stalin), were representative of this group.

In addition, a group of Russian-language officers would also play a key role in American foreign policy from 1943 and especially after 1947. Bill Kelley of the State Department trained a generation of Russian specialist foreign service officers who included George Kennan, Charles "Chip" Bohlen, Loy Anderson, Llewellyn E. Thompson, and others.

While the former group (the elite northeastern lawyers and bankers) was more influential during the war, the latter group (the Russian-language specialists) would emerge as the most significant advisers to President Truman after the war, and especially to his secretary of state, General George C. Marshall, as well as Marshall's deputy and later secretary of state Dean Acheson.[1]

The most articulate and therefore most prominent of the Russian specialist foreign service officers was George Kennan, who served as a third secretary to ambassador to the Soviet Union Joseph E. Davis (1938–39) and as chief counselor to ambassador to the Soviet Union Averill Harriman (1944–46). Kennan wielded considerable influence over Harriman and possibly was the author of the most significant memos sent by Harriman to the president. Kennan was notorious for his skepticism, distrust, and disdain of the Soviet state. The most succinct of Kennan's ideas were articulated in two significant pieces. The first was the famous long telegram (eight thousand words) which he sent in 1946 from Moscow to Washington. This message impressed Secretary of Defense James Forrestal so much that he distributed copies to all significant members of the administration. Secretary Forrestal was possibly the father of the Cold War, but intellectually he was inspired by George Kennan, who supplied him with ideas for the formation of an American policy toward the Soviet Union.

The second item, possibly one of the most influential written on American Soviet policy, was the one Kennan wrote in *Foreign Affairs* (July 1947) under the pseudonym "Mr. X." In this essay Kennan set out his philosophy of political realism and his understanding of Soviet behavior as a guide for educating American elites (governmental, educational, journalistic, political) about the nature and structure of Soviet behavior and conduct in foreign affairs. In both the long telegram and the Mr. X article, Kennan emphasized that the Russian rulers suffered from "instinctive insecurity," that the sources of Soviet foreign policy were internal, and that American policy should be "long and vigilant containment." Kennan also emphasized that the Soviet leadership understood the limits of its seemingly boundless military capacities. The threat from the Soviet Union was not military, it was political, intellectual, and psychological. As a realist, Kennan believed national security and national interest must guide American interests. Therefore, a partnership with the Soviet Union was out of the question, not so much for ideological reasons, because as a realist Kennan did not consider Soviet ideology's influence on foreign policy. But the nature and structure of the Soviet state and its rulers precluded any American national interest in a partnership with the Soviet Union. The American national interest dictated that there was no reason, or hope, for cooperation with the Soviet Union as advocated by President Roosevelt and his advisers because, to paraphrase Kennan, the two nations were separate, not at par with each other. Ideology, according to Kennan, was no guide for action. It is employed only to justify action. The United States should not seek a partnership with this revolutionary state because the Russian state and Russian society were isolationist and Russian nationalism, rather than communism, guided Russian foreign policy. American interests did not converge with these aspirations. With the policy of containment Kennan sought to strengthen "our society," "our diplomacy." Above all, the national interest would dictate an Atlantic relationship; it was the industrial states that were America's natural partners. Therefore, he advocated a policy of support and recovery for Europe, especially Germany, and also for Japan.

Kennan was neither a democrat nor a liberal (the word "democracy" rarely appears in his writings); he was an elitist. He wanted foreign affairs to be run by a platonic intellectual elite. A careful reading of his interview with George Urban in *Encounters with Kennan* reveals that his ideas were reactionary. He sought a return to some form of Jeffersonian rural, peaceful, nonmodernist universe.[2] There was, however, no more articulate individual to relate the essence of the Cold War than Kennan.

Kennan's strategy as it related to the Cold War involved restoration of the balance of power and abandonment of Wilsonian universalism. George Kennan abhorred Wilson's and Roosevelt's foreign policy. Roosevelt seemed to him an amateur. According to Kennan,

> Until the final days of his life, Franklin Roosevelt seems to have clung to a concept of Stalin's personality, and of the ways in which the latter might be influenced, that was far below the general quality of the President's statesmanship and reflected poorly on the information he had been receiving about Soviet affairs. He seems to have seen in Stalin a man whose difficult qualities—his aloofness, suspiciousness, wariness, and disinclination for collaboration with others—were consequences of the way he had been personally treated by the leaders of the great European powers. FDR concluded that if Stalin could only be exposed to the warmth and persuasiveness of the President's personality, if, in other words, Stalin could be made to feel that he had been "admitted to the club" (as the phrase then went)—admitted, that is, to the respectable company of the leaders of the other countries allied against Germany—his edginess and suspiciousness could be overcome, and he could be induced to take a collaborative part in the creation of a new postwar Europe.[3]

To Kennan, Woodrow Wilson seemed a romantic fool, naive in diplomatic and realistic policy. Kennan, with Hans Morgenthau and Reinhold Niebuhr, became the representatives of political realism challenging the concept of national interest that dominated the moral and legalistic aspirations of both Presidents Wilson and Roosevelt. In that sense, the Russian expert foreign service, graduates of observation of Stalinism and international communism, who were maliciously ignored by President Roosevelt during the war, flourished under the Truman-Marshall-Acheson administration.

Kennan's strategy called for the fragmentation of the international communist movement. Kennan opposed military challenges to the Soviet Union and felt that they were unnecessary. Kennan felt the United States could use economic and psychological means to play a key role in helping to fragment international communism and certainly to prevent another state or regime falling prey to Stalinism. American strategy should be based on diversity and an international policy that did not advocate universalism. Kennan served as George Marshall's first national security adviser, and he surrounded himself with a group of talented foreign service officers who became his intellectual policy "think tank." The function of the foreign policy planning staff was to formulate and develop long-term programs for the achievement of U.S. foreign policy objectives. The Policy Planning Staff (PPS) defined the national interest in international affairs as follows:

1. to protect the security of the nation, by which is meant the continued ability of this country to pursue the development of its internal life without serious interference, or threat of interference, from foreign powers; and
2. to advance the welfare of its people, by promoting a world order in which this nation can make the maximum contribution to the peaceful and orderly development of other nations and derive maximum benefit from their experiences and abilities.[4]

As an advocate of the Atlantic community, Kennan also stretched America's interest to include the Mediterranean oil centers, Japan, and the Philippines. The major exercise for containment was, to paraphrase Kennan, to modify Soviet international conduct, not for purposes of a partnership with the United States but to bring about a negotiated settlement of the outstanding differences between the United States and the Soviet Union. The key to containment was a long-term economic policy and European recovery. Western Europe was of great significance for American national interest. Kennan's tenure as PPS director did not last long, however. The new secretary of state, Dean Acheson, chose the more aggressive and militant Paul Nitze as Kennan's replacement.

Paul Nitze, of course, is famous for drafting NSC-68, which became the bedrock and foundation of American Cold War policy. First and foremost, it called for the creation of institutions to deal with the Cold War. One must remember that the United States fought the greatest war in its history without a central bureaucratic authority, except for the president. There was no White House staff, only presidential surrogates such as Harry Hopkins and Averill Harriman. The State Department was ignored as sort of a nineteenth-century diplomatic beehive of striped-pants diplomats. The institutions and organizations that proliferated in Washington during the war demonstrated a lack of administrative, political, strategic, and diplomatic coherence. The United States, by fiat, emerged from isolationism into a monumental, complex, all-encompassing world war. It was not only unprepared intellectually and politically but lacked the necessary security and strategic institutions for the conduct of the war. There was no defense department; there was a War Department and a Navy Department. There were no national security offices or strategic coordination in the White House or elsewhere. Strategic intelligence did not exist in the Roosevelt administration. Only late in the war, 1944–45, did Colonel Bill Donovan, under the president's instruction, organize a secret intelligence agency known as Office of Strategic Services, which played a more important role in supporting anticommunist, social democratic, and Christian democratic parties in Italy, France, and Germany after the war. This lack of security organizations had to be corrected under the Truman administration once the United States entered the Cold War. Thus such institutions as the National Security Council, the new Defense Department, an independent air force, the Joint Chiefs of Staff (a legacy of the war reinstitutionalized), and above all intelligence organizations such as the CIA and related security organizations were formed to fight the Cold War. The Policy Planning Staff had been an innovation of the Cold War, which gave the Department of State an intellectual and policy headquarters to generate ideas that could influence the president and other administration officers. The State Department absorbed the Office of Strategic Services, the Foreign Economic Administration, and other disparate institutions created during World War II to coordinate the economics and the strategy of the war. The State Department was "largely neglected and was ineffective, whose morale was exceedingly low."[5] Kennan was enthusiastic about becoming "deputy secretary of state in charge of ideas" and, above all, about lifting the Department of State from the ignominy of the dismissive Roosevelt and the arrogant secretary of state James F. Byrnes.[6] In the Marshall-Kennan State Department, ideas and action converged under the brilliant administrative reorganization of General Marshall, who brought to the department his experience as an army chief of staff and as a chief of the American-British Joint Chiefs of World War II.

The Marshall Plan demonstrated that the major American thrust, next to the security of Europe, was economic, a neo-Wilsonian New Deal, new mercantilist international diplomacy. Not unlike the New Deal, economic recovery and the Marshall Plan were to establish a new economic order, restructuring the world economy along the corporate order and, in many ways, duplicating the New Deal economic and social corporations. European economic recovery was essential to the long-term American interest.[7] The Marshall Plan was a neo–New Deal effort to impose an American economic order as the source for European recovery. This was harkening back to Secretary of State Cordell Hull's (1933–44) idea of a boundaryless economic system in which states would play a secondary role to economic institutions and structures. This was the basis for the formation of the International Monetary Fund and the World Bank, American-created institutions in the American corporate image for an American Century.

The first American effort to stabilize Europe was providing

aid for its economic reconstruction. This was clearly epitomized in the Marshall Plan. This effort was followed by, and later linked with, the Atlantic Defense Treaty (ADT) and also involved a domestic debate over the use of American troops in Europe. President Truman prevailed in keeping a permanent American force in Germany. NATO was, of course, a consequence, conceptually and politically connected with European economic recovery. This was a perfect effort on the part of the United States to reestablish the balance of power in Europe, to restore order, to ensure stability, socially, economically, and militarily. The balance of power followed, as the balance of terror and the implementation of a nuclear umbrella in 1954.

The North Atlantic Treaty Organization was created in 1949, the first European security organization in which the United States had a permanent presence. NATO would become the center of American policy and strategy in Europe. It was the first time the United States would enter European politics and security, no longer "on the cheap." The United States would provide not only the political and strategic leadership for European security but also an American nuclear umbrella. The era before 1945 seemed medieval in comparison to the second half of the twentieth century.

The dividing line between the first and second halves of the twentieth century is significant for its impact on American foreign policy and its role in European, Soviet, and world affairs. Between 1945 and 1950 the United States enjoyed a monopoly on nuclear weapons, but even after this imbalance was corrected by the emergence of the Soviet Union as a nuclear power, the United States would continue to be the leading Western superpower in international politics. No longer would the United States turn back to the isolationism or neoisolationism of the past. This past seemed remote by the standards of 1950 and later. Henry Luce called the twentieth century the American Century, but this was mainly true for the second part of the century. The foreign policy and concept of international order of Truman, Marshall, Acheson, and Kennan was no longer ideological. It essentially followed power politics but as always with a neo-Wilsonian vision.

This time, ideology justified the neorealism of American security and foreign policy. The concept of security, unknown in the first half of the twentieth century, became the quintessence of American policy in the second half of the century. This time, it would not be a new world order but an American world order. No longer did this order share space with another international system, it was *the* international system. It was neither a new nor an old order but an international system dominated by the United States but challenged by the emerging European military superpower, the Soviet Union.

Containment, by itself, was an insufficient strategy. Its implementation required military strength. Paul Nitze's PPS NSC-68 moved Kennan's vision forward, and soon the two of them would debate the relative virtues of atomic and conventional deterrence. The Cold War could not be formulated and implemented in an abstract world. The distinction between military and political containment was good enough for Kennan's purposes, but with the formation of NATO and the emergence of the Soviet Union after 1950 as a nuclear power, an abstract containment policy was no longer valid. Kennan opposed NATO and reluctantly accepted American intervention in Korea. He advocated a unilateralist strategy. He saw Korea as a blatant Soviet provocation. Kennan's formulation of containment was inconsistent and unclear, especially as it related to militarization; in later years he not only denied the need for militarization but condemned it. Nitze's NSC-68 embodied much of what Kennan opposed regarding the militarization of containment. Kennan opposed the globalization of containment, and in later years he would become the chief spokesman against the United States acting as a global policeman. Kennan did not accept the intellectual and strategic role of nuclear weapons in the Cold War. He rejected the use of nuclear weapons for strategic and diplomatic purposes. He still belonged to a pre-1945 generation in this respect. Paul Nitze became the advocate of the strategic importance of nuclear weapons, and their elimination became an important foreign policy goal. At the time Nitze wrote NSC-68, he was no advocate of nuclear weapons, and he had doubts about the usefulness of tactical weapons. When Nitze took over the NSC in 1950, the idea of nuclear deterrence and nuclear rivalry was still far off on the horizon. According to Jerald A. Combs, both Nitze and Kennan "might have formulated a containment policy less drastic than the one that emerged from NSC-68 and might have compromised on a less strenuous conventional arms-building program."[8] The chances were slim that Nitze or Kennan would have agreed on the NSC-68 policy if they had been completely responsible for it. Combs tells us: "First, Nitze underwent a temporary conversion from his view of the limits of atomic deterrence. Second, Kennan presented his notion of conventional deterrence and Soviet capabilities even more ambiguously than he had previously put forward his ideas about the military and global limits of his containment policy. To a great extent, the view of both Nitze and Kennan on conventional arms was a function of their attitudes toward atomic weapons."[9]

Paul Nitze was not as horrified at the role of nuclear weapons as Kennan. Already as a member of U.S. Strategic Bombing Survey in 1945 he was aware of the consequences of the bombing of Nagasaki.[10] But Kennan, writes Combs, "opposed a conventional arms buildup to compensate for the loss of America's atomic superiority."[11] Although Nitze is certainly identified with the militarization of containment, "he even acknowledged the inevitability of a nuclear stalemate and the dangers of relying on the use of atomic weapons. Accordingly, like Kennan, he concluded that it would be logical to rely more heavily on conventional deterrence."[12] NSC-68 was connected to the decision whether to test the feasibility of a hydrogen bomb.[13] For both Nitze and Kennan, American security depended on maintaining the balance of power, but for Nitze it meant a delicately poised balance and hence was known as the balance of terror, much as Paul Nitze tells John Lewis Gaddis "on the *perception* [emphasis added] of the balance of power as on what that balance actually was."[14] Kennan's perception was always based on limited resources and his inflexible attitude that the Soviet Union had no interest in war. Nitze did not see the Soviets as malleable. He advocated a "symmetrical response" policy, which meant that the

United States would act wherever the Russians chose to challenge its interests. This was a serious departure from Kennan. Nitze became an advocate of nuclear power later. But he was alarmed when the American military trumpeted the dangers of Soviet atomic weapons. The rise of nuclear weapons would also change Kennan's early advocacy of abandoning cooperation with the Soviets, especially in Germany, and of building separate Western spheres to contain the expansion of the Soviet Union. After the Marshall Plan had succeeded in stabilizing Western Europe, Kennan did foresee cooperation with the Soviet Union in the nuclear era and an effort either to abolish the weapons or to effect a mutual withdrawal of troops from Germany. Kennan called for the neutralization of Germany and Eastern Europe, which of course was rejected by Nitze in NSC-68.[15]

Fundamental differences separated George Kennan and Paul H. Nitze as directors of the Policy Planning Staff. Nitze's NSC-68 was a comprehensive statement on the future of American policy. According to Gaddis, "One of the most striking things about NSC-68 is its perception of the international order. Like Kennan, it saw American security as dependent upon the maintenance of a balance of power, but unlike him, it perceived that balance as delicately poised. Kennan had argued that there were only five meaningful centers of power in the world—the industrial complexes of the United States, Great Britain, the Rhine valley, the Soviet Union, and Japan—and that as long as no more than one of these was under hostile control, international equilibrium would be preserved."[16] For Nitze, the maintenance of the balance of power was not as critical as the dangers of Soviet intimidation and humiliation that would damage the United States's credibility. The power of the United States in the world "was critical to Nitze."[17] The two men differed over the *perception* of the balance of power, not the actual balance of power. NSC-68 suggested ways to increase the defense budget and expenditures without war. Its prescriptions would strengthen American military power as a deterrent rather than using the psychological-economic means of deterrence in Kennan's doctrine. NSC-68 stated that "the integrity of our system will not be jeopardized by any measures, covert or overt, violent or non-violent, which serve the purpose of frustrating the Kremlin design."[18] "Frustrating the Kremlin design" became an end in itself, not a preparation for war between the superpowers. NSC-68 set American containment policy on the path toward making the fragmentation of the international communist movement a long-term goal. It broadened the limits set by Kennan regarding military expenditures and the eventual militarization of containment. The test of NSC-68 was, of course, its implementation. The North Korean invasion made President Truman agree to endorse NSC-68.

Perhaps the most important development connected with NSC-68 was that American official thinking as formulated by Truman's advisers preferred the military rather than the diplomatic strategy which was represented in U.S. nuclear deterrent policy in dealing with the Soviet Union. Thus the strategic and ideological divide became deep and uncompromising in the late 1960s and early 1970s. The Cold War was set in stone and became an ideology in itself.

The Cold War demonstrates the prevailing ideology of collective defense and the Wilsonian concept of American liberal exceptionalism combined with the Truman-Acheson ideological realpolitik. In the Cold War, the United States for the first time became deeply involved in the most successful and long-lived military coalition in the twentieth century, defying the long-held American foreign policy principle of intervening briefly and on the cheap. With the exception of the Cold War, Wilsonian American foreign policy following World War I was marked by reluctance to become militarily, economically, and strategically involved in other nations' affairs or in international politics in general. But the Cold War, NATO, European recovery, and Europe as the central front became an American responsibility. The U.S. nuclear umbrella was offered to protect Europe and deter Soviet aggression. A Soviet nuclear attack on Europe would have caused an American retaliation, which would have led to a Soviet counterstrike. For the first time U.S. foreign policy was linked to the fate of other nations, and the violation of European stability could result in serious damage to the United States. The Cold

War was a policy *not on the cheap*. Not only did the United States accept financial burdens and station troops permanently in Europe but it would be as much an object of Soviet aggression as Europe. This linking of fates between the United States and Europe was more than exceptional; it was unique and therefore out of character with American foreign policy generally in this century. Despite proclamations of American responsibility for a new international world order, the United States before and after the Cold War refused to pay the price required to link it to other nations and states, some of which had national aspirations that were in contradiction to those of the United States. Nevertheless, the Cold War was conducted on a high moral and ideological plane, which was politically meaningful, and an American national consensus was established around the fight against the "evil empire."

World War I brought an end to the classical European balance-of-power system. World War II restored the balance of power, although it became a nuclear-based balance of terror governed by the United States and the USSR with Europe and NATO as second players. The sweeping changes since the age of Wilson in world politics had been monumental. FDR and Stalin, the latter very reluctantly, established a new organization to ensure peace, the United Nations, a more forceful version of the League of Nations buttressed by the European-oriented Security Council and powerful and consistent American participation. In the war against fascism, Nazism, and Japanese radicalism, both the United States and the USSR were the victors. Britain and France were relegated to a subordinate role, and Germany was divided and occupied.

The new international order was *not* created, dictated, and finalized at Teheran, Yalta, Potsdam, and Dumbarton Oaks. After 1945, the new and awesome ultimate weapon, the atomic bomb, would hold the key to war and peace. Possession of the ultimate weapon would dictate the power relationship between East and West. The clash between democratic forces and Marxist totalitarianism would divide the world far beyond the traditional, classic boundaries, territories, and military concerns. Between 1945 and

1949, even though the ultimate weapon was exclusively in the hands of the United States and the West, Stalin continued to occupy, Bolshevize, and consolidate his control of Eastern Europe. Only in the battles for Greece, Turkey, and Korea was the communist hegemonial onslaught stopped by the use of conventional force.

In a sense, neo-Wilsonianism and neo-Leninism were locking horns on a huge scale. In the first phase of this conflict the West held the nuclear monopoly; the second phase became known as the hard Cold War. The superpower balance-of-terror system was different from any seen before in history, driven by the presence of the chilling but stabilizing new super weapon. The struggle was between two coalitions, each claiming ascendancy over Europe and the newly independent postcolonial states. This new order was not governed by a sense of mission, by idealistic urges, or by visions of class or racial utopias, although the struggle would often be clothed in ideological garb.

The new international order was designed to tame the bomb. The unintended paradox of history is that had the bomb not been used against Japan, providing vivid evidence of its destructive power, the balance of terror might have been even more frightening. Uncertainty and ignorance of the bomb's actual power could have very easily escalated into nuclear warfare. Although there have been scholarly and journalistic efforts, fifty years after the atomic bombs were dropped on Japan, to claim that the war could have been won with minimal casualties and without the use of the bomb, Harry Truman was correct in deciding to shorten the war.[19] An unintended psychological and strategic consequence of Hiroshima and Nagasaki was the world's awareness of the devastating annihilatory power of nuclear weapons, which set the tone of the state of mind concerning nuclear power ever since. This ultimate and awesome weapon is prohibitive as an instrument of policy, even if Eisenhower, Kennedy, and Nixon, as well as Khrushchev and Brezhnev, willingly made political and strategic use of the bomb, short of its actual deployment. This does not mean that there were no nuclear war scares, but the balance of terror clearly demonstrated the efficaciousness of the bomb. Without Hiroshima and Nagasaki, it might not have had this effect.

The existence and use of the ultimate weapon had a sobering effect on post–World War II statesmen and diplomats. The new balance of terror was in part psychological. The overpowering image of the atomic cloud hung over the international system during this period, and its destructive darkness had the ironic and salutary effect of securing a relatively stable international order.

In many ways, this was an ideal, if sometimes tense, international order, rational, pacific on the whole, except for bursts of small wars by those who challenged or tried to manipulate the new order. Even though the rhetoric and language of the times were occasionally aggressive and bellicose, stability was maintained. In addition, the great powers and their allies rearmed to an extent and at a pace, level, and volume of potential destructiveness unknown before in history.

This system, in spite of its rhetoric, did not augur well for democracy or promise freedom. The Cold War proved that only superpower alliances could guarantee peace, that the most awesome weapon of all would be the source of stability, and that military alliances within the two blocs—NATO and the Warsaw Pact—would be the guarantors of stability in the region.

The Western alliance was *not* an effort to create a universal order of democracies and self-determination. The struggle between the two great powers and blocs, reminiscent of the days of the old European power politics, was conducted on the peripheries, outside Europe, in the arena of former colonies that were now confused, erratic, and vulnerable independent states seeking their own forms of mutual security.

The realization of the consequences of an all-out or even limited nuclear war restrained the leaders of the leading blocs in the United States and the USSR. Mutual distrust and misperception prevailed but did not upset the system or lead to a nuclear war. The weapons contributed a conundrum that assured stability: the price of war was too catastrophic; it very possibly would cause total annihilation, and there would be no winners. There was a paradoxical quality to these times. To remember the often violent, challenging, and threatening rhetoric put forth by both sides during the period, one would believe that nuclear war was certain to take place at some point. Yet peace prevailed right up until the collapse of the communist system and the Soviet Empire, which was brought about without recourse to war. Not that there were not some hair-raising, fearful moments. In the 1962 Cuban Missile Crisis and the 1973 Arab-Israeli War the super powers came close to nuclear war.

The Cold War was a Faustian bargain between the United States and the USSR, a kind of unspoken pact to conduct a rivalry without ever using the ultimate weapon. In "The Delicate Balance of Terror," Albert Wohlstetter examines, "because of its crucial role in Western strategy of defense . . . the stability of the thermonuclear balance which, it is generally supposed, would make aggression irrational or even insane. The balance, I believe, is in fact precarious, and this fact has critical implications for policy."[20] In the words of Wohlstetter, the delicate balance of terror gave the United States choices in a nuclear strategy which were "hard" and must be "responsibly made." Wohlstetter revolutionized the American nuclear strategy. His ideas were offered to mute the jeremiads of the time who claimed that mutual extinction could be the only outcome of war. In fact, Wohlstetter proved the prophet when he said that it was because of the nuclear balance of terror, delicately managed, that a major war between the superpowers was avoided. A nuclear balance of terror was nevertheless a true balance between hegemonial powers that were not essentially equal except militarily. The Soviets had more people and military might, but the United States was always economically and technologically stronger. The USSR was a military power, but the United States was both an economic and a military-technological power.

For almost fifty years, international peace reigned, twice the period of peace between the two world wars. It was a period not governed by utopian schemes or "new" world orders designed for peace or conquest. The dangerous mania for pacts that characterized the period between 1919 and 1939 was missing. The making and acquisition of lethal weapons increased until the number of missiles carrying nuclear bombs from land, sea, and air was awesome and redundant.

From 1950 to 1989, the concept of security, as embodied by NATO and the Warsaw Pact, was mixed with balance and power. It was principally a conscious and sustained American policy. The struggle against Stalinism, Soviet and communist totalitarianism, became the cornerstone of American foreign policy whose major effort would be directed at containing Soviet imperialism or expansion in the Third World.

Hans Morgenthau, a dispassionate, hard-nosed political realist, argued that the Cold War was a struggle for hegemony, plain and simple. Others have argued that the Cold War showed that the United States was not dedicated to the concept of collective security. America's Cold War policy mixed ideology and realism. Thus the Soviet Union could be seen simultaneously not only as a foe of American democracy and of freedom, the ideological wellspring and flagship of communism, but also as an expression of Russian imperialism that predated communism.

Containment was essentially a policy of realpolitik, a modern version of the balance of power pursued in various ways by Presidents Truman, Eisenhower, Kennedy, Johnson, and Nixon. It always had aspects of a moral crusade, but it was also the ultimate form of realpolitik as it strove for a balance of terror instead of helping create a new democracy or defending old ones.

Bipolarity was the new world order. In a world dominated by two hegemons, not the United Nations or any world of nations would become the center of U.S. politics and policy because the United States was at the UN's center, as FDR had hoped. When FDR died and the Cold War set in, the last of the old Wilsonian spirit vanished. Deborah Larson is correct in saying that the arguments of the realists in turning away from Wilsonian precepts were couched in psychological terms such as "taming the Russian bear." Russia's failure to "keep agreements," "getting tough on Russia," and the almost demonic figure of Stalin were all rationales for abandoning the unrealistic tenets of Wilsonianism.[21]

Stalin did not manage to intimidate the United States and Europe, but he did lay the seeds for the Western-American perception of the Soviet Union held by all presidents since Truman. Even Jimmy Carter, when confronted with Soviet aggression in Afghanistan, abandoned his more idealistic or Wilsonian instincts in favor of Cold Warriorism.

There is no question that the Wilsonian legacy of democracy and self-determination cast a long shadow over U.S. foreign policy concepts, and to some extent still does in the Clinton era, but it is rooted more in philosophy than in action. The Wilsonian vision of an ideal world order, however, especially as embodied in the United Nations, has turned sour because that organization has been dominated since the 1970s by African and Third World kleptocrats and Arab praetorians and the communist bloc empire before it was seriously diminished. Much of this was more related to the end of colonialism than to ideology. Perhaps not surprisingly, the Third World turned away from the West and the imperialist powers. In 1955, the Bandung Conference of nonaligned nations, dominated by Jawaharlal Nehru, Marshall Josip Tito, and Nasser, raised the specter of an entirely new moral world order. On the surface, it was the kind of bloc or grouping Wilson would have supported, but Nasser and Tito not only failed to provide an example of moral world order but also turned their regimes into nightmares of coups, civil wars, countercoups, and police states. Chou En-lai, who participated in the conference, together with Mao Tse-tung, headed the world's second totalitarian state. Nehru, the only democrat among the nonaligned nations, failed to chart an alternative moral and international order. The nonaligned nations gamely tried to play East against West but ended up witnessing the political and moral collapse of their own regimes and their vaunted attempted at so-called order. In a way, the rise of this group and its brief moment in the sun demonstrated Wilsonian precepts at their most wrongheaded, with the concepts of democracy and self-determination turned upside down. Self-determination, the motivating force in a postcommunist Europe, has become a tool for establishing nondemocratic statism and authoritarianism in the Third World.

The driving force of self-determination in the postcolonial

Sub-Sahara, in the Middle East, and in Latin America became a handmaiden of authoritarianism and a scourge for democratic structures and impulses. The postwar world was decidedly not safe for democracy. Yet in a larger way, the postwar world *was* safe because of the fear of the ultimate weapon and its capacity for total destruction. Power politics and the preponderance of power would replace Roosevelt's world order. The crowning glory of Roosevelt's successor, Truman, was the creation and installation of a postwar vision that replaced FDR's vague and unrealistic neo-Wilsonian vision with a European-American Atlantic alliance—the Marshall Plan.

What historians once described as Truman's "creative peace" was a search for European integration, and it succeeded. This was the Western world's order, stable, enduring, and prosperous. It has outlived the communist utopia, Stalin's aggression, Third World decrepitude, and any number of short-lived political passions.

When historical states and common cultures share a commitment to freedom, democracy, economic development, and free enterprise, a basis for world order can be built and maintained. Hitlerism, Leninism, and Third Worldism have all failed. These movements and ideologies were never truly international in spirit and could not be exported beyond regional and national borders as ideas with shared values. They were either superimposed, by conquest or treaty, or contained too many principles and ideas that did not take into account their own limits and practicality.

Self-determination and democracy are not necessarily coexistent values, and they are not without inherent and dangerous contradictions. Security and stability have proved more sustaining than the drive for self-determination.

In essence, the successful world order rested on the belief that the recovery of Europe was crucial to U.S. interests. This was a grand departure from Wilson's universalism and FDR's collective security, his Four Policemen scheme for a new world order. This was a regional Atlantic order of the industrialized democracies which could better protect, supervise, and guide the world toward peace and security than the United Nations collective security regime could. NATO, following a multination European defense and collective security strategy, negates the idea of a universal collective security system embodied in the United Nations. After failing to establish a grand strategic policy for the United States after the war, Roosevelt resorted to a neo-Wilsonian collective security system strengthened by the idea of the Four Policemen, which became the Security Council of the United Nations. It was a concert of powers on one hand and collective security on the other. In the end, neither one worked, and they were replaced by the two nuclear hegemons, who established the balance of power and peace. Examination of any serious conflict since 1945 will clearly demonstrate the futility and irrelevance of the United Nations and the naiveté of the principle of collective security. The United Nations was characterized by gridlock, and it became largely irrelevant whenever the Soviet bloc colluded with the Third World blocs against the United States and the Western European bloc. Not much has changed since the end of the Cold War.

The nuclear balance of terror, combined with a regional alliance based on culturally and politically shared values, proved to be the right combination for a new, stable, more peaceful world order. NATO turned out to be the major and most effective foreign policy and security creation of the United States and its European allies. Its purpose was to serve both as a bulwark and an alarm against communist aggression in Europe. NATO was a limited collective security organization whose purpose was to maintain the balance of power. European recovery was linked to a military and cultural alliance. In this way, the new concept of Europe was doubly represented, in NATO and in the United Nations Security Council. The force behind NATO was the permanent and symbolic but also very real deployment of American troops in Europe, which reassured Europe that the American commitment was serious.

Another purpose of NATO was to fashion a United States of Europe. This concept was attacked by Marxists from the left and isolationists from the right. The Marshall Plan was Wilsonian only in the sense that it became a democratic regional order and served as a military bulwark against communism. It was an Atlantic world order, economically, militarily, and politically. It was Rooseveltian in the sense that it resembles the New Deal in linking private enterprise to government. Although the Marshall Plan seemed in some ways a quintessential New Deal project, its basic goal was political and strategic, as Michael Hogan put it, "to forge a Western European bloc of nations of sufficient size and coherence to withstand the dual dangers of Communist subversion and Soviet aggression."[22]

The Cold War brought about the longest era of peace in this century. There were no world wars for over half a century. The question is how much it was inspired by Wilsonian ideals. At the end of World War II, discussions of Wilsonian principles were revived with the founding of the United Nations. Wilson certainly was an internationalist and committed to a peaceful world order. Yet as an American nationalist he exhibited a narrow outlook, as demonstrated by the Versailles Treaty and the punitive measures imposed by the Allies, which he accepted. Wilsonianism also put limits on American intervention. Frank Ninkovich writes, "The half-life of America's enthusiasm for collective security lasted barely a generation and decayed so rapidly thereafter that American internationalism bore scant resemblance to [Wilson's] vision of world order based on the League of Nations."[23] This is undeniably true, but Wilson cannot be taken literally. Conceptually, Wilsonianism is a theme running on and off through American foreign policy in the second half of this century. Power politics to create a balance of power has always been rejected by the United States body politic. Nevertheless, Wilsonian moralism allows the United States to act in world politics in a way that a strict moral order would not. The Cold War is a perfect example of this type of Wilsonianism. It did not preclude the deep moral and ideological commitment for a nation that was literally born out of a grand idea. Therefore, the Cold War could be conducted only under an umbrella of ideological persuasion that could provide American diplomats with good consciences and a realist outlook. American diplomats and the American public are apprehensive of forging a realpolitik foreign policy. Therefore, it is preferable to

American foreign policy makers as well as the president to combine the worldviews of Woodrow Wilson and Teddy Roosevelt. The Cold War was the most representative and successful blend of the two. The "cold" meant that the "war" would become violent unless limited by nuclear deterrence, which would guarantee the cooling of passions. In fact, the Cold War represented American ideals and international reality, and the Cold War consensus supported what actually was a realpolitik diplomacy. This means, in a Machiavellian sense, that preparing for war is the best way to keep the peace. During the Cold War the American president clearly projected America's hegemonial economic, political, and military power. Even if the sociology of the struggle was Wilsonian, it was Teddy Rooseveltian in the sense that above and beyond the ideological struggle, it was also a cultural rivalry that was settled finally only when the rival Leninist system became exhausted and decayed and its ideology and institutional arrangements came to their logical end.

Much has been said and written about Wilson's Christian-Protestant cultural orientations, although it is doubtful that either he or his successors were committed to a Christian-Protestant political weltanschauung. Rather, they articulated a sincere provincial decency, extraordinary for a great power. The Cold War had to be graphically and rhetorically demonstrated as a struggle between good versus bad, Reagan's "evil empire," a Spielbergian supersatanic Hollywood farce. Even though Wilson's League was short-lived, the precedent of intervention in Europe, of casting international law and morality along this Faustian procession, certainly makes the Cold War a Wilsonian event.

Wilson never advocated the end of power. But power was to be an instrument for good to eliminate evil. To be beneficent, power must be held by a well-meaning, highly moral leader, who represents the best of liberalism, democracy, and capitalism, which to Wilsonians are the virtues of the United States and in its national interest. The protection of these institutions can supersede boundaries and can legitimize intervention. A nation of immigrants, pluralistic, representative, a civil society that holds human rights sacrosanct, must be defended, if necessary by intervention and war. Since Wilson, FDR, Carter, and Clinton have represented this view of America. In the most recent American intervention in Bosnia, Clinton spoke of America's reasons for sending American troops to defend the Balkans: intervention is the "right thing to do." "From our birth, America has always been more than just a place. America has embodied an idea that has become the ideal for billions of people throughout the world. Our founders said it best: America is about life, liberty, and the pursuit of happiness."[24] He went on to say, "In this century, especially, America has done more than simply stand for those ideas, we have acted on them and sacrificed for them. Our people fought two world wars so that freedom could triumph over tyranny." What a quintessential Wilsonian sermon. Yet how could the president do otherwise, as a realpolitiker, an individual who would claim "a plague on all your houses," or, as George Kennan wrote many years ago, to leave the new emerging nations to the mercy of their self-interest? An American president must ride the white horse, armed with Wilsonian rhetoric. The Cold War presidents Truman, Eisenhower, Nixon, Reagan, and Bush had less prosaic rhetoric and more pragmatic action. The Cold War as foreign policy, to paraphrase Walter Lippmann, was the shield of the republic.

The Cold War was portrayed by revisionists as an instrument of the power elites, a conspiracy of the ruling classes dominated by a corporate triangle of business, labor, and the universities.[25] It was a creation of a cabal of white Protestants, scions of the eastern establishment, trained in elite universities, World War II veterans, especially of the intelligence institution, the OSS, and its successor, the CIA. In this view national security becomes a state by itself and the Cold War is dominated by a network of men who succeeded in creating consensus among the American people and Congress based on their deeply rooted anticommunism.[26] This is actually a caricature that fails to demonstrate how the left hand of the cabal wrestled with its right hand; members of the cabal were rivals and competitors, whose approaches ran from that of George Kennan, who believed in psychological and historical containment of the Soviets, to Secretary James Forrestal and Paul Nitze, who believed that containment required American militarization. For this group, according to neo-Marxist American intellectuals and academics of the New Left, the Cold War was an American war. To the New Left, Stalin's hegemonial and imperialist orientations and deeds meant very little, for in the end Stalin was more a figure (not an innocent one) acting in the power elites' Cold War than taking initiative in it. Not that Stalin was weak by any means, not that he was not malicious and ruthless, but Stalin had no intention of destroying the European system or challenging the United States militarily. Thus the Cold War has assumed a life of its own. To the Marxists it was the highest stage of capitalism, substituting imperialism for Leninist-Luxemburgian classless utopia. The view of the New Left critics of the Cold War was reinforced by neoisolationists and those senators who hoped the United States would stay out of Europe's international wars. The critics of the Cold War are reminiscent of the fin-de-siècle pacifists, anti-imperialists, and feminists, in the United States, as well as others who believed that war must be ended at any price and that international institutions such as a league for peace must be installed so that war could not occur again. Wilson's world order was antirevolutionary before and after the Russian Revolution of 1917. The United States, a revolutionary country at home, became the preeminent antirevolutionary power in international politics. The Cold War represented this antirevolutionary American orientation because it was an American-sustained balance of power hitched with ideological, anticommunist, antirevolutionary slogans, which were necessary to persuade Congress and the American people of America's righteous role as the bulwark against revolutionary communism. Realpolitik was rejected as an old European concept that was wrong. Therefore, the Cold War had to be conducted in the shadow of an American diplomatic culture that concealed its realist procedures. Indeed, it was a success. The American system prevailed, and the revolutionary system collapsed. What next?

CHAPTER 7

The Kremlin's Cold War after Stalin

The USSR lost the Cold War. Stalin's drive westward was halted by the United States and its NATO allies. Stalin's efforts in the Pacific and his deep involvement in the Korean War—which he helped to instigate—were frozen at the Thirty-eighth Parallel. The pure imperialist designs had come to naught; yet the post-Stalinist Soviet policy remained anchored in communist ideology. The arena for Soviet ideological maneuvers became the former colonial world, the Third World. Once the effort to make use of communist parties to subvert the prevailing regimes in France and Italy came to an end because of covert American political and financial support of democratic forces (most conspicuously in Greece, where a CIA-dominated government was established), the arena shifted to the Third World. Here ideology became the instrument of hegemonial expansion. Marxist and communist theories had considerable appeal in Western Europe. When Mao occupied China these ideas seemed the wave of the future, beginning with peace movements and other Cominform-inspired subversion. An effort to capture the minds of Western and Eastern liberal intellectuals was rebutted by the American CIA-supported front organization, the Congress for Cultural Freedom.

The Soviet Union could pose as a liberator, the force that brought an end to Nazism and fascism. The Western nations were painted as capitalist plutocracies, dominated by American corporate capitalism. The "progressive" Soviet Union represented the wave of the future. Thus hegemonialism and realpolitik became enveloped in ideological Marxist rhetoric. The Soviets' real interventionist aspirations were couched in utopian discourse, placing the United States on the defensive.

The containment policy was misperceived by Stalin and his successors as an American drive for supremacy in Europe, as Western aggression, just the opposite from what George Kennan conceived it to be. As several authors have demonstrated, this Soviet reaction was a mixture of fear and paranoia. The Soviet sense of insecurity that bred the Cold War also provided the constraints that kept it within bounds. This is not to say that the threat the West perceived was an empty one. In the quest for security, Stalin and his successors were inclined to take greater risks whenever they saw the trend of events turning in their favor. In estimating their own strengths and the weaknesses of their adversaries, they were prone to miscalculations. Their confidence was enhanced by their ideological preconceptions, which postulated the ultimate victory of their system despite temporary setbacks.[1] Thus post-Stalin leaders attempted to create buffer zones, neutral areas, with a united neutral Germany as the crown jewel in that arrangement. The hope was that a united neutral Germany would bring about the dissolution of NATO and end the American presence in Europe. The Soviet goal was to keep American troops out of Europe, or as far from Soviet borders as possible. NATO troops acting as an alarm bell were perceived by Stalin and his successors as an indirect threat to the Soviet Union. The removal or distancing of these troops, which would take place once a united Germany was neutralized, was the essence of Soviet countercontainment policy.[2]

Also significant in the resolution of the Cold War were American nuclear superiority, the Soviet challenge to it, and the Soviet perception of the nuclear balance of terror. As David Holloway clearly demonstrates in his work *Stalin and the Bomb*, Stalin did not appreciate or clearly understand the role of the ultimate weapon.[3] He remained moored in pre-1939 international politics and in his belief in the importance of military forces, and the victory against the Nazis persuaded him that large divisions were the instruments of hegemonial power and the only deterrent forces against aggression. But Lavrenty Beria and Georgy Malenkov, the former the atomic czar of the Soviet Union, had a better perception than Stalin of the importance of nuclear weapons. Stalin and his successors were dedicated to catching up as fast as possible and to establishing some sort of parity with the West regarding nuclear weapons. This called for a monumental effort, brilliantly and thoroughly described by Holloway, by a variety of means. Accelerated research, investment of vast sums for nuclear and missile development, the creation of a republic of scientists and scientific works related to the military beyond the Ural Mountains, and a concerted spy and theft network of atomic and scientific information from the West (i.e., the United States and Great Britain, the two powers that developed the atomic weapon) were all undertaken to enhance Soviet nuclear development.

In missile development, the Soviets outpaced the United States, as they did in space exploration. Sputnik created panic in the United States, and Soviet missile development became a central national and foreign policy issue for both the Eisenhower and Kennedy administrations, known as the "missile gap" controversy. This fear spurred American acceleration of missile development and resulted in the mad armament race that took place in the 1960s and 1970s and continued until the demise of the Soviet Union.

As Vladislav Zubok and Constantin Pleshakov state, there was no unanimity among Stalin's successors as to how to meet the Western challenge—containment and the bomb.[4] There was no debate under Stalin; he personally conducted Soviet foreign policy with the aid of his subservient lieutenant Molotov. But after Stalin's death in 1953, there emerged a rivalry between his successors Molotov, Andrei Zhdanov, Beria, and Malenkov. Molotov was a prisoner of the Stalinist weltanschauung. Like Stalin, he believed that Russian power and Marxist ideology would prevail. The policies of Zhdanov, who helped resuscitate the old Comintern (now called Cominform), were directed toward integrating and dominating the Eastern bloc so that the Cominform could speak with one voice issued from Moscow. Beria and Malenkov were creatures of Stalinist terror. Both played key roles in the Stalinist purges, in the Stalinist Gulag system, and therefore were under the shadow of the policy that they and Stalin had instituted (especially Beria, who survived his own purges). Both were involved in military industrialization, and Beria's fundamental role in the development of the Soviet atomic industry and capability was to continue with his setting of an atomic policy. The bomb obsessed Beria and Malenkov. Thus Stalin's successors' responses to his Cold War policy did not speak with one voice.

As Zubok and Pleshakov correctly write, Beria and Malenkov learned to love the bomb. They began to understand its political implications more than Stalin ever did. But the collective leadership of Molotov, Malenkov, and Beria, although under the veneer of a Malenkov primacy, was transitional. The person who in my view had the greatest influence on the Cold War between the rules of Stalin and Gorbachev was the mercurial peasant Nikita Khrushchev. According to Zubok and Pleshakov, "Nikita Khrushchev inherited the Cold War from Stalin, but his impact on its course was as legendary as his legacy in every aspect of Soviet life. His flamboyant personality, style, and beliefs help explain the most serious crises in United States–Soviet relations that held the world in suspense and finally brought it to the brink of nuclear war."[5] Khrushchev campaigned to wind down the Cold War but created the opposite, a sharp increase in world tensions. Why?

Khrushchev represented, more than Stalin, the dichotomy between a Russian imperialist and a Soviet revolutionary. There was little question that Khrushchev romanticized the Russian Revolution. Yet in the classical Russian tradition (even if he was a Ukrainian), Khrushchev more than any of the other oligarchs of the Soviet Communist Party and state was a world-class statesman. He had more imagination and flexibility than the perennial foreign policy czar under Stalin: Molotov. The trouble with Khrushchev was that he was unpredictable and volatile, highly emotional. "Khrushchev firmly believed that the USSR had been wronged, mistreated by the United States after the end of the

Second World War."[6] Khrushchev put the onus of responsibility for the Cold War and American-Soviet confrontation on the United States. But as Zubok and Pleshakov state, "Much of Khrushchev's engagement in the Cold War can be explained by his desire to overcome Stalin's entangled international legacy and by his confidence in his ability to outfox the 'dark forces' in the United States."[7] And he rejected "the inevitability of global war." As a Soviet revolutionary, however, he believed in the historical inevitability of the collapse of capitalism; it would collapse on its own rather than through military confrontation. On Khrushchev's trip to the United States, he claimed that "we shall bury you." What he meant was that capitalism was doomed, and the triumph of communism was inevitable.

Khrushchev accelerated Soviet acquisition of the ultimate weapon in the belief that the bomb would be a deterrent force, as Western policy makers considered it to be. Because accelerating Soviet missile development would enable it to challenge the United States in a nuclear confrontation, he could proclaim his desire for "peaceful coexistence" with imperialism and capitalism hoping that in time capitalism would collapse. Peaceful coexistence was a countercontainment idea. Unlike the American containment policy, it was not systematic or clearly articulated and had no intellectual underpinnings. It was an emotional, pragmatic formula for the bomb to serve to deter the West while the internal contradiction of capitalism brought about its demise.

Khrushchev was the first Soviet statesman to proclaim a balance-of-power theory of international relations. Stalin's thinking, as demonstrated by his relationship with Roosevelt and Churchill, was moored in the balance-of-power universe. Khrushchev raised this policy to an intellectual level, if one can call it intellectual. But unlike Stalin's, Khrushchev's policy was based on prudence and caution. Khrushchev's policy was tested in two prominent and major international crises of the Cold War: the Berlin blockade and the Cuban Missile Crisis.

Whether the Berlin crisis was created on purpose or accidental, it certainly was related to the German problem. One cannot understand European politics since 1919 and certainly after 1945 without paying attention to the German problem. Germany is the crucible between East and West; American or Soviet foreign policy toward Europe is founded on the role assigned to Germany. Certainly Konrad Adenauer's West Germany, with its membership in NATO, its clear Western democratic orientation, and its growing economic power, posed the most significant challenge and threat to Soviet security interests in Europe. Zubok and Pleshakov write that ever since the middle 1950s, "Soviet diplomacy in Germany had aimed at consolidation of the status quo and sought a balance between deterrence of Bonn and support of the GDR's sovereignty on one hand, and attempts at rapprochement with the FRG against the GDR's objections on the other."[8] "Peaceful coexistence," eventually detente, and certainly the efforts to neutralize Germany were the central post-Stalinist Soviet countercontainment policies. The Berlin crisis stemmed from these apprehensions and considerations.

The refusal of the United States to accept the Soviet German peace settlement and the Soviet belief in the decline and death of capitalism made Khrushchev decide to gamble in Berlin even though he knew how firm Washington felt about Berlin. The Berlin crisis was a typical Khrushchevian affair, unpredictable, volatile, seemingly unreasonable, and simply threatening—an effort to notify the West that as long as the German problem was not solved the Soviet way, the stability of Western Europe was not guaranteed. For Khrushchev, Berlin was realpolitik in the sense that a clear struggle for the balance of power was going on in Europe, and that balance would be precarious unless the German question was solved as he wished it to be. President Eisenhower and his advisers decided to fight in Berlin. According to Zubok and Pleshakov, based on research in the Soviet Union after its fall, Khrushchev viewed Eisenhower as a "sober and peaceful man."[9] Like earlier Soviet rulers, Khrushchev had only a crude understanding of the United States; he saw it through Marxist glasses. Like Ambassador Litvinov in the 1940s, Khrushchev believed the United States was divided between two forces: eastern capitalists with a liberal orientation (represented by the Rockefellers) and aggressive, crude capitalism (represented by the American West, a sort of caricature of a John Wayne movie).[10] If Litvinov thought that President Roosevelt was surrounded by advisers friendly to the Soviet Union (such as Harry Hopkins, Ambassador Davis, and Mrs. Roosevelt), Khrushchev perceived Eisenhower to be a member of the eastern liberal establishment in opposition to reactionary forces (such as the CIA, the radical right of the Republican Party, and the Texas oil millionaires). Eisenhower, he felt, was a good man. After all, after the deaths of Stalin, Churchill, and Roosevelt, Eisenhower was the most important living figure of World War II. Stalin had always spoken highly of Eisenhower, as a great general, a friend of the Soviet Union, a great statesman, a man of peace. Khrushchev would discover how greatly he had misperceived Eisenhower, one of the toughest realpolitikers and American Cold Warriors, who "disappointed" Khrushchev's illusions. Soon enough he would discover that Eisenhower was made of steel, and his Berlin gamble collapsed.

It is the cunning of history that the first post-Stalin Soviet leader—who wanted to bring an end to the Cold War and hoped for balance of power and peaceful coexistence through the creation of buffer zones to enhance European stability—was the man who exacerbated Soviet-American relations, as both the cases of Berlin and Cuba demonstrate.

The case of Cuba is an even more tragic story for Khrushchev. As he had believed in Eisenhower as a partner, Khrushchev now had faith in the new President Kennedy, a young man not tied to historic American anticommunism and not rooted in the Cold War establishment. Again, Khrushchev was rudely awakened. According to Zubok and Pleshakov, "For the first time he [Khrushchev] was to deal with someone not anchored to a set of hostile, preconceived notions about the USSR and the Russian revolution," but he badly miscalculated.[11] The first Soviet leader to have the courage to denounce Stalin and Stalinism, even though he had to amend his statements later, the first Soviet ruler to act in grand manner in the international arena, the first noncloistered Kremlin Politburo apparatchik, Khrushchev was a disappointment to himself and threatened international stability. His miscalculations, nuclear brinksmanship with Kennedy over missiles in Cuba, and a misperception of the West's position on Berlin almost brought about (with the cooperation of President Kennedy) a nuclear confrontation. Thus a flexible Soviet policy as an effort to overcome containment and the nuclear superiority of the West did not act as a deterrent, as Khrushchev had hoped it would. His policy toward the colonial world, which has been known as the "new outlook," was nothing but an unvarnished Stalinist attitude. But unlike Stalin, he was not shy about intervening in the muddy political waters of the Middle East and Sub-Saharan Africa. His pernicious role in support of Pan-Arabism and Nasserism, which brought him into conflict with Ba'athist Syrian nationalism and made him a prisoner of Arab aspirations and a victim of Arab-Israeli wars, did not augur well for the man some Western analysts have called "the great peacemaker."

Stalin would never have had the confidence in revolutionary imperialist dual policy, the idea that linking hegemony and ideology would bring a Soviet victory, that Khrushchev did. Stalin could contain his revolutionary zeal with a heavy dose of political realism and a natural talent for playing the game of power politics. Stalin was more stable, less of a visionary, a product of the Russian Revolution and its consequences, whereas Khrushchev, although romanticizing the revolution, failed to enhance Soviet security and the balance of power because his use of ideology was faulty, especially when dealing with the Third World, as his fiascoes in Egypt and Syria demonstrated. In the case of Germany, he was a total failure. Rather than ameliorating East-West relationships, he made them more rigid. He left a more belligerent legacy to his successors. Khrushchev's successors, through Gorbachev, did not exactly return to Stalinism (this was no longer possible), but they did return to imperialist interventionism, which brought them no relief and no stability. Leonid Brezhnev in particular, an unimaginative Politburo communist apparatchik, made no initiatives toward easing East-West relations. As the case of Afghanistan demonstrates, Khrushchev's successors seemed to have learned nothing from his miscalculations.

Because the security of the regime was most important to the post-Khrushchev generation of Soviet rulers, they maintained the status quo. This paradoxically opened the gates for arms control negotiations, treaties, and understandings, a process that had begun under Khrushchev. The Soviet Union joined the nuclear balance of terror even though it occasionally demonstrated old revolutionary imperialist tendencies and interventions. The stagnation and decay of the Soviet political and economic system was a flagrant demonstration of the false illusions of Khrushchev's Soviet march into the future. What took place after Khrushchev was not only stagnation but a retreat to a universe dominated by competing Soviet political administrative and military factions, each carving for itself gigantic economic and political territories, a situation that partially exists now in Russia; different *nomenklatura* dominated different economic, political, and military functions and resources. The Politburo game is a sort of consensus of the division of labor between the different dominant and aggressive *nomenklatura*. Until Gorbachev, a sort of peaceful coexistence was in place among the various forces. Foreign policy was a function of who had more influence in the Kremlin. Most of the time it was the military and security services, as the foray into Afghanistan demonstrates. At other times, it was the arms controllers, as was demonstrated by the long and arduous Soviet-American arms negotiations.

The Brezhnevite Soviet Union changed the U.S. perception of the Cold War, bringing to the fore people in the Democratic Party center and center-right, represented by Senator Henry "Scoop" Jackson, many of whom would obtain key defense and security positions in the Reagan and Bush administrations. The Committee for Present Danger was made up of people who would play prominent roles in the Reagan administration. While the Nixon-Kissinger detente was failing because of an inadequate response from Moscow under the procrastinating Brezhnev and his successors, a new Cold Warrior group emerged led by Paul Nitze, Richard Perle, Jeane Kirkpatrick, Max Kempleman, Richard Pipes, and Scoop Jackson Democrats, who, with support from magazines such as *Commentary* and *National Interest*, formed a formidable foreign policy establishment that played a key role in formulating the Reagan policy of starving the Soviet Union and encouraging the United States to undertake the largest and most elaborate arms and defense expenditures in this century. Although the neoconservative anti-Soviet Reagan policy makers claimed that his administration won the Cold War, there were internal pressures as well that caused the Soviet Union to fall. The failure to establish the so-called workers' utopia demonstrated that Lenin's and Stalin's ways of combining communism and the state were ultimately detrimental to the state and its rulers. Furthermore, Gorbachev, realizing how the Soviet Union was decaying, tried valiantly but unsuccessfully to implement perestroika policies. Nevertheless, the Reagan group's military buildup must have persuaded the Kremlin rulers that they could not continue in the arms race. History does not have just one explanation, but to dismiss the role of the Reagan administration in enhancing the collapse of the Soviet Union is ahistorical. The Cold War was not made of one cloth. If one analyzes certain aspects relating to the ideology and hegemony of the Cold War, American hegemonialism won and the Soviet Union disappeared. The Reagan administration's policies helped to hasten the downfall of the Soviet system. If Brezhnev and his successors Constantine Chernenko and Yuri Andropov until Gorbachev had lived longer, maybe the Soviet Union would not yet have collapsed, even if it was in a process of accelerated decay. One must give Gorbachev tremendous credit for realizing that the die had been cast against the old system and that without serious political, economic, and administrative reforms, the Soviet Union would cease to be a hegemonial power even though it was the second nuclear power in the international system. Hegemony does not mean that a state has to use its military power; it has to project power. Even a corrupt and decadent Soviet Union was in a position to wield power and did so successfully throughout its history. But Gorbachev understood that hegemony, without a powerful and efficient industrial system and a powerful economic base, cannot subsist on military and nuclear power alone. The decline and corruption of communist ideology, not apparent to former colonial parties and rulers, was nevertheless an obstacle to Soviet hegemonialism. If after 1945 communist ideology enhanced the projection of Soviet power, it ceased to do so toward the end of the century. The interrelationship between ideology and power and the sustenance of the hegemonial role had been prominent parts of the history of the Soviet Union.

The United States can exist without an interventionist ideology, although it showed itself to be an interventionist power in the Greco-Turkish crisis, the Berlin crisis, the Berlin Wall, the Cuban Missile Crisis, and the Vietnam War. But in a democracy, unlike a totalitarian system, ideology cannot be a purpose of foreign policy. American covert operations and interventions were antagonistic to American democratic and moral values and anathema to the originator of covert action: Woodrow Wilson. The American pretense that it was intervening to save democracies in Vietnam or elsewhere was defeated by the American Congress and people. Presidents were defeated. But a mission-oriented America can survive even if the mission fails, as the demise of Wilsonianism several times over demonstrates. Yet during the Cold War, the ideology of anticommunism, democracy, and the free market provided the cement for the Western alliance; in some sense it was the essence of the Western alliance. In the 1930s America could not have played the role it played in the 1940s in Europe because of American isolationism and the combination of power politics and ideology. The Atlantic Alliance was created not only to sustain the balance of power but to reinforce values, which some may call ideology. This does not mean that the United States did not intervene in the most brutal fashion in Latin America and the Middle East, in coalition with the most reactionary and praetorian radicals, making an American claim of democracy a sham. Certainly the Reagan policy in Latin America did not demonstrate a grand victory for democracy. But with regard to the Soviet Union, the situation is completely different. The state and the ideology were so organically intertwined that the demise of one brought an end to the other. American democracy persists, even if the United States brought to power Latin American and Middle Eastern revolutionary and reactionary dictators. The American body politic is not dependent on foreign policy; it has a life of its own in the sense that the presidents of the United States represent either the center-left or the center-right. The American dream continues to be a domestic aspiration of all political parties. The exportation of American ideals, Wilson-style, could solidify the American hegemonial role but did not make the body politic dependent on it. In the Soviet case, however, Stalin and his successors, especially Khrushchev and to a certain extent Brezhnev, understood only that the materialistic, deterministic universe was a property of the Soviet state and empire. Ideology, however distorted, however crude, however irrelevant at times, was a fountainhead for Soviet power. It justified Soviet aggression, intervention, expansion, or retraction. It was a glue that could give the regime, internally and externally, the right to rule. Soviet hegemonialism without communist ideology could not survive. Even if neorealists argue that it was nuclear power and security that protected and defended Soviet hegemonial power, communist ideology was a fundamental ingredient of Soviet security. To dismiss ideology as irrelevant is to misperceive the nature and structure of the Soviet Union from Lenin to Gorbachev. The structural argument of neorealism must incorporate, in the case of the Soviet Union, the significant role of ideology, the foundation of the regime, its purposes, its historical and international role. What would Russia be without communism? Certainly a nuclear power and perhaps even an ally of the West. But there would have been no Cold War. The Cold War was not merely an adjustment of the balance of power between two hegemonial rivals; it was also a war anchored in ideology as security. This is conclusively demonstrated by the behavior of the Soviet Union, from Stalin to Brezhnev and to a certain extent Gorbachev. The ideological basis of communism, which Gorbachev claims to believe in (maybe in more reformed, social democratic ways), was essential to the sustenance of the Soviet regime since the days of Lenin. Soviet foreign policy and its role in the Cold War reflected this organic relationship between hegemony and ideology. In an age in which unvarnished imperialism is no longer tolerated internationally, when national sovereignty is the essence of independence and security, the intervention or occupation of other peoples must be done "voluntarily," that is, through a "people's revolution" which, with the aid of the hegemonial Soviet Union, would bring to power its revolutionary party and leaders. In 1945, the nationalist communist coalitions became communist totalitarian dictatorships in Eastern Europe; the opposition was quashed by the use of security forces. When ideology is no longer believable domestically, the security services must institutionalize ideology as the internal security of the state and in foreign affairs the security of the Soviet Union and its supremacy. This was the function of the international communist movement before and after the war, when all communist parties in the world were completely subservient to Soviet foreign policy. The Soviet Union was proclaimed as the mother of communism and progressivism and thus able in the name of ideology to dominate regimes and states without being identified as an atavistic imperialist. The external Soviet Empire could be interpreted and perceived as a liberating force rather than imperialistic and atavistic (to use Schumpeter's idea of classical imperialism).

CHAPTER 8

A "New" New World Order?

What can be said of the post–Cold War era of stability? Obviously the rise of two cautious and prudent atomic superpowers played an important role in the stability of Europe. Some authors would dispute that the powers were either cautious or prudent. At the same time, they would argue that the effectiveness of weapons made states behave with caution and prudence. Certainly the bomb made a difference. Global war became unthinkable, which was the major lesson that the ultimate weapon taught in harnessing uncontrolled aggressions and passions.[1] Aggressive violation of international peace was replaced by the balance-of-terror system to guarantee stability and peace as well as the unacceptability of the status quo. Contrary to the Wilsonian aspiration, it was rearmament which, among others, was responsible for the defeat of Nazi Germany and defended the West during the Cold War under the nuclear umbrella. The greatest rearmament of all time took place between the two superpowers, and the longest peace occurred under a nuclear shield. Between 1919 and 1939, the mania for pacts between small states, not involving empires, destabilized the international system. Aggressive rearmament during the Cold War contradicted the belief that military power is responsible for warfare. It was successfully employed as a deterrent power. Woodrow Wilson intervened in World War I, making possible the Allied victory but violating his principles and commitment. An arms competition during the Cold War was replaced by the concept of sufficiency, that is, the saturation of weapons and treasure, which in the end did justify a policy designed to meet Soviet aggression and establish stability. It can certainly be argued that Reagan's sustained and energetic military procurement and rearmament policy was one of the reasons for the collapse of the Soviet Empire. It certainly was more effective than Nixon's detente or Carter's coming to terms with the Soviet Union. But it overspent and overreached the objective. Yet one can argue as Machiavelli did several centuries ago that diplomacy, stability, and peace can be achieved only by vigilance and military readiness. The Cold War confirmed Machiavelli's concept of peace, that it was not the absence of weapons but the fear of the powers of an atomic Armageddon that was more responsible for peace than all the peace movements combined.

The great era of peace since 1945 was not owing to elimination of weapons but to the strategy of deterrence, which governed the behavior of the superpowers. The ultimate weapon played a tremendous role in creating the stability that sustained the peace. It is likely that Woodrow Wilson would have supported the American Cold War policy, for it protected not only the integrity of the United States but also its principles. The bloc struggle between 1948 and 1963, which is known as the classic Cold War (or the first phase), could have erupted into a world war if not for the deterrent effect of the bomb. It was not just democracy that defended democratic regimes, but rather it was their military sufficiency. The international order did not require American exceptionalism to flourish; it required military hegemonialism to persuade the belligerents of the intolerable cost of an all-out war. Despite the dire predictions of pacifists and realists, there was no World War III. Certainly the ideological divide could have been a serious threat to international security, but it did not evolve into a catastrophe. Nor did international goodwill, tourism, festivals, Olympics, international institutions, or cultural proximity and integration stabilize the world. These efforts could not have prevented a world war, especially because of the high ideological tensions. Nor could the naked neorealistic rationalization for establishing stability with a minimum of nuclear weapons and systems. The new and sophisticated nuclear arms control system, the mechanisms, and above all the universality that came from the bomb sustained the post-1945 system. The United Nations or universal collective security, which at best played a supportive role subject to the goodwill of the superpowers, did not achieve what the greatest rearmament of all times did. This is not a paradox; it just confirms the concept that the insecurity of nations stops at the threshold of use of the ultimate weapon. The old concept known as "security dilemma" was reintroduced to the debate over who won or lost the Cold War. As Jacob Heilbrun writes, "At its heart is the old idea developed in the controversy about the origins of the first world war, that arms races are not caused, but are themselves causes; that they have their origins in an 'action-reaction' phenomenon; and that wars result accidentally from the very steps that nations take to avoid them, and to ensure their security."[2]

The search for a new world order is culturally and ideologically an American preoccupation. The old world order means a non-American world order, old to the Americans in the sense that it is tired, cynical, pessimistic, quarrelsome, with a limited horizon. In contrast, the American order is optimistic, expansive, hopeful, humanitarian, democratic, liberal, pacific, and open-minded. Thus when the "evil empire" passed away, when the good won against the bad, American foreign and security policy makers were left in a quandary. Bush's war against Saddam Hussein was still a war against a bad guy. The support for Somalia was on the cheap and ended as a fiasco. What has really occurred is that the U.S. foreign policy makers, their analysts, and their detractors have all sought an evil to replace the Soviet Union, something bad to kick around. Unfortunately for proponents of a new world order, classical and historical international conflict has returned in the form of ethnic conflicts, border disputes, religious fundamentalism, and terror. What is missing is a grand strategy. Unsuccessful efforts have been made, both before and after serious violence occurred, as in Bosnia and Haiti. The pundits and analysts attack the Bush and Clinton administrations for their failure to design an overarching foreign policy, although they do not ask themselves, What for? Some are passionate about an American doctrine. James Webb, secretary of the navy in the Reagan administration, argued that the United States has confused the missions and purposes of its armed forces, that it is reactive. He argues that the United States needs to formulate a grand strategy for its armed forces to achieve its purposes in forthcoming conflicts. Are these the last gasps of neo-Wilsonianism, as is the case of President Clinton's intervention in Bosnia? Once again the argument becomes almost completely moral and Wilsonian, intervention on the cheap. So there is no way to extricate the dream of a new world order from an American foreign policy, even to paraphrase Alice in Wonderland—the cat is gone, the smile remains, and it is inexplicable but not completely. Different euphemisms for the new world order are being introduced in the elite press and foreign affairs magazines. They advocate policy for the twenty-first century, the end of the current system of hegemony and bipolarity. And, of course, the emergent neorealist school analyzes everything from the structure of the international system to hegemonial relationships—or the absence of such relationships. The international system is governed by power politics. The relationship between hegemony and ideology and power politics is necessarily introduced once again to understand international behavior as well as to explain it and probably to predict it. With the United States now the single superpower or hegemon, these neorealists see very little threat and very little role for the United States in the Haitian, Bosnian, and Somalian conflicts. General Colin Powell, the former head of the Joint Chiefs of Staff, created a strategy based on the preponderance of power, the "Superior Force Doctrine," a strategy for deployment of the U.S. armed forces because the American military is not only the best in the world but the most efficient, professional, and technologically superior, the only armed forces that could tip the political or military balance for grand strategic purposes. U.S. armed forces command, control, and coordination of the navy, the air force, and the super technology demonstrated in the Gulf

War are a sufficient deterrent to the only challenges to American power: the rogue states. Therefore, one does not have to exercise oneself too much about a new world order and all the Wilsonian language attached to it. Of course, until a new hegemon rises to challenge U.S. security, a world order that is dominated by a single American hegemon guarantees that the probability of a world war is low. Nevertheless, American security does not require it to intervene and become involved in the affairs of mini-states. Such action is needed only when American national security is threatened. Thus an aggressive nuclear North Korea, Iran, and Iraq, a return to an undemocratic regime in Russia, or a belligerent China would require American intervention. The ethnic wars in the Balkans do not require American vigilance. However, the end of the Cold War does not absolve the United States from international responsibilities even when not fortified by an ideological purpose.

What is the future of the new world order? Is such an order required? The Cold War as a balance-of-power–balance-of-terror system may have come to an end, but the intellectual policy debate over war and peace is only beginning to churn into high gear. Since 1989, there has been a huge volume of written and spoken words on such issues as the so-called new world order, the replacement of geopolitics by geoeconomics (a vacuous term), and whether such old concepts as isolationism, interventionism, bipolarity, and multipolarity are still useful and meaningful. In all this verbiage and debate, a serious confusion over the meaning of foreign policy and international politics has arisen, which needs to be addressed and clarified.

It was not until the French Revolution that such ideological concepts as mission and modern nation-state international systems came into being. The French Revolution was an all-encompassing, international event that threatened the stability and integrity of nonrevolutionary empires, the then existing hereditarian systems in Europe. Thus the concepts that appeared to be embodied in the French Revolution—republicanism, democracy, and egalitarianism—were perceived by the post-1815 statesmen as revolutionary forces that would destabilize the European system. This era was dominated by conservatives who established the classical balance of power among conservative, stable, and nondemocratic states in defense of the monarchies. Metternich and Talleyrand designed a foreign policy, an international-oriented system, to defend the integrity of the monarchy against revolutionary forces.

As the great scholar Quincy Wright wrote some fifty years ago, international relations amount to a "condition"[3] in which antirevolutionary, antimessianic regimes and a system to defend those traditional states and the status quo in society, politics, and the intellectual arena are established. International relations meant the management of power in which a majority of sovereign states defended the status quo and the balance of power.

Hans Morgenthau, probably the most prominent student of international relations and foreign policy, also wrote half a century ago that power politics is political realism. The main tool that helps political realism to find its way is the concept of interest defined in terms of power.[4] Interest is the center of foreign policy, and foreign policy is designed to negotiate, manage, and defend national interest. In other words, narrowly defined, national interest overrides international missions and revolutionary aspirations.

Systematic foreign policy is the management of power which, ever since the French Revolution, has followed all revolutionary upheavals. In the aftermath of World War I, Woodrow Wilson sought to create a world safe for democracy. This was to be an American exceptionalist world and an international order of republics and democracies that would bring an end to militarism, imperialism, war, and, above all, revolutionary Bolshevism, which had been unleashed by Lenin and the communist Soviet Union. Lenin envisioned foreign policy in Marxist terms, against the background of a classless, revolutionary world subservient, of course, to the cradle of the revolution, the Soviet Union.

Lenin and Hitler, with his Third Reich racial world order, revolutionized the international system in much the same way that the French Revolution and Napoleon revolutionized Europe 125 years earlier. After the destruction of Hitler, U.S. foreign policy responded to the new totalitarianism of Stalin's Soviet Union, by following a new mission—the ideological containment by diplomacy, propaganda, and military means of communism in Europe, Asia, and other arenas.

The Cold War world was characterized by rivalry between two nuclear superpowers in a contest of ideology and power that resulted in a balance-of-terror–balance-of-power system. Foreign policy became an antirevolutionary force and tool for the United States, Western Europe, and democracies in general. Interest in this arena was defined not only by power but also by ideology and a sense of mission. The equally mission-oriented (but traditionally imperialist) Stalin had to be contained, restrained, and put on the defensive lest another revolutionary movement—communism in its Stalinist expansionist guise after 1945—threaten to destroy the stability of the status quo powers.

Now that the ideological and political mission of the Western powers has been fulfilled, a mission-oriented ideological rivalry no longer exists, and the international system is once again without order, in a state of flux. But it is oriented toward maintaining the balance. Foreign policy should now be reoriented and be conducted on the basis of national interest, extended to maintaining a regional balance of power and preventing nuclear proliferation, without ideological commitments, cementing power and the raison d'être for intervention.

There is really no new world order because there is no revolutionary mission or rival hegemonial threats to the system, only regional state-ethnic conflicts in a world order dominated by one hegemonial power. The lack of a new world order is actually a hopeful and pragmatically positive state of affairs because it implies the absence of a zealous, threatening, destabilizing force to preoccupy the conduct of foreign policy.

Of course, the international system may from time to time be disrupted by localized violence, but such conflicts do not have the potential for disrupting an international system. They can, however, produce remarkable ad hoc coalitions designed in the short term to put an end to aggression, as for example, Desert Storm or the U.S.-NATO coalition to bring an end to the Bosnian war. But the United States, as a sovereign and stable nuclear superpower, an economic giant, will pursue a foreign policy, not some nebulous new world order or global utopia. The idea of a new world order is charged with missionary zeal and must be avoided for the more mundane but critical and pragmatic issues of states, regions, economics, and environment. In other words, the United States will eventually distance itself from missionary and messianic ideas of world order, which collapsed with Wilson, Lenin, Hitler, and the Soviet Union. A new world order means a new tyranny—although a moral one—and foreign policy means sanity, the practice of defending the sovereign states in a given international system. The secularization of foreign policy without a mission does not mean an end to hegemonialism, power, or intervention.

What, then, is the shape of the "newest" world order? President George Bush could hardly qualify as a scholar of international politics, but he was an experienced practitioner of war and diplomacy, the last of the old-style Cold War presidents, who coined the phrase "new" world order to define the post–Cold War era. By this he meant the end of totalitarianism and the spread of democracy and free markets to the former Soviet Empire. It was actually a disguise for American hegemonial conduct in international politics.

The post–Cold War world is neither Wilsonian nor ideologically free. There was a pragmatic quality to Wilsonianism, even though it was an example of the conduct of American foreign policy. In fact, there is no "new" world order, one that is pursued by a grand morality. To begin with, there is as yet no governing balance of power. If there is something approximating a world order, it is a regional political and economic order at best, made up of groups like the European Economic Community (EEC), the Pacific Rim, North American Free Trade Agreement, and others.

There can be no identifiable world order unless *there is one*. The new world order has no prophet, no compass, no leading international actor to help establish or sustain it like Hitler, Lenin, or Wilson. A dying neo-Wilsonianism—Clinton style—is hardly a clarion call for an international order of the sort characterized by that which existed between 1919 and 1939. Nor is there a superpower balance of terror such as that of the Cold War world between 1946 and 1989.

The governing ideology since the end of the Cold War has been nationalism, ethnicity, and Moslem zealotry. The urbanization of the world into a global village created by the communications revolution is oriented toward long-standing struggles over patrimony and identity, of which Georgia and Yugoslavia are chief examples. Following the melting of the Soviet totalitarian glacier, little democratic grass has grown. Rather, tribal, patriotic, nationalistic, and ethnic forces are trampling the old ground, some aggressive, others benign. Nationalism and ethnicity can never serve the interests of international order.

The European cultural and economic community must be nourished until the new *visograd* Central European states of Poland, the Czech Republic, Hungary, and possibly Slovakia are stable. What exists today is not a nineteenth-century balance of power restricted to Europe. What remains after the Cold War is an Atlantic Alliance with an unclear mission; who is the enemy, what is the mission? But because it was successful politically and became an organic part of the European cultural, economic, and political system, the military alliance should not be abandoned. The United States as a hegemonial power must maintain its troops and play a key role in the Atlantic Alliance, even though there will be no unity of purpose and mission as there was against the Soviet Union. The case of Bosnia demonstrates divisions within the alliance, which will probably persist in other conflicts. Nevertheless, because there is no guarantee that a new hegemonial power will not emerge in the twenty-first century and to recreate NATO once it is abandoned would take monumental efforts (and might not succeed), it is in the interest of international security—and above all European security—that NATO be sustained. The argument that NATO should be enlarged is not valid, even if it will happen by 2000. A conflict may occur between Turkey and Greece, two NATO powers, because an Islamic-oriented party may gain power in Turkey. But NATO has faced Greek and Turkish differences over the issue of Cyprus before. Neither one opted to leave NATO because the alliance did not support them. In short, it would be a political mistake of enormous magnitude not to sustain the military alliance system called NATO. If NATO is turned into a multiplicity of unequal powers and its estimated expenses are not tolerated by the budget-conscious American Congress, however, its projected $2.5 billion budget deflates in seven years. An ancillary argument could be made that the expansion of NATO, which will have to include the *visograd* states, would be enormously expensive. Just think of trying to modernize their decaying military so that it can become an effective part of NATO. Why destroy an effective military organization that has served us so well since 1949? Rather than expanding NATO, the European Community should be expanded, for unless American, European, and Russian interests converge, the idea of NATO expansion is an exercise in futility that has become Clinton's major European endeavor. There must be a political way to ensure the security of the newly liberated Eastern European states without antagonizing Russia. Unless there is a genuine, all-inclusive European Community, this time without a Soviet threat, there can be no benefit from expanding NATO. The European political community, still far from complete, and the European security community are no substitutes for the military alliance and for the psychological, political, and strategic position NATO has achieved and projected. In politics, deterrence of any form means projecting the ultimate capabilities of power, not the real operational ones. And NATO as a threshold for European security must, should, and will continue. Russia has an option, to enter or not to enter NATO and the European system. Russia must understand that NATO's mission today is not as a bulwark against Russia, unless it resorts to its historical imperialism, but rather to serve as a European shield, of which a more stable Russian regime could become a part. As political events are developing in present Russia, there is no guarantee that either it or Europe is yet ready for one another. This does not exclude Russia from joining the European Community. Whether Russia is democratic or not is not relevant. What is relevant is that the regime be stable and that the historical imperialist aspirations of czarist Russia are being gradually abandoned.

The present trend is against the establishment of a new world order to keep international peace and tranquillity. What strategy, then, should the United States, the only remaining nuclear superpower, pursue in the wake of the peaceful disintegration of communism everywhere in Europe and the USSR?

A U.S. strategy should include working for free trade and movement of peoples and goods; a capacity to maintain a military posture that would check serious international disorder as it did in part during the Gulf wars of the 1980s to 1990s, which means protecting the Gulf states from Iraq and revolutionary Iran; defending South Korea as long as the North Korean regime remains belligerent; challenging the radical regimes of Iran, Iraq, and North Korea; keeping a permanent U.S. military presence in Germany to guarantee the stability of East-West relations; and preserving the balance of power in Asia. American policy makers and planners should consider China a potential hegemonial power, if not economically, certainly militarily, and policy should be established based on realistic facts, not on Wilsonian utopian dreams of imposing American values in the form of an aggressive human rights policy on the most populated state on earth.

The United States will be the only remaining hegemon at the beginning of the next century. The EU and the Pacific Rim are serious potential regional political and military structures. Neither China, Japan, nor Germany could be, at least for now, a hegemonial power. They successfully compete economically with the United States. But they are politically and militarily linked to the United States as hegemon, and Japan and Germany particularly continue to depend on America to secure Europe and the Pacific. NATO may or may not expand to the East. Russia may or may not become a democracy in the twenty-first century. Neither European nor Asian countries except China could affect the world order or advance an ideology or purpose that can establish China as the center of a new world order. The prevailing order for the next century is the United States's order. The United States still possesses the only power of international veto. Why otherwise would it become involved in Somalia, Bosnia, or Haiti? The idea of free markets and political liberalism is well entrenched in Western Europe and East Asia and now spills over into Eastern Europe and Latin America. A new world order as an idea can exist only if Wilsonianism is the driving force of American policy. A great misconception on the part of President Wilson was that the evolution of democratic regimes would lead to a peaceful international order. No such evidence has been seen in this century. World War II was won by overwhelming American economic and military power and brutal Soviet resistance to Hitler. The Cold War was won by the predominance of American economic and nuclear power. Neither had to do with democracy; even the legitimacy of the weaker Western powers and their loyalty to the alliance rested heavily on democracy. The only democratic states created since World War II were Spain and Portugal after the 1970s. Greece and Turkey are borderline. Ukraine, Poland, Hungary, and the Baltic states aspire to become democratic. The Czech Republic has crossed the road to democracy. The Moslem republics of the former Soviet Union resemble more the Arab Moslem regimes, characterized by authoritarianism and praetorianism. Latin America is still divided between new democracies and lingering praetorian and authoritarian regimes. The world is not ready for democracy. But this does not mean it is not ready for political stability. The objective of a "world safe for democracy" does not automatically make the world safe. Democracy is not a requirement for international peace and order or for domestic tranquillity. After all, the totalitarian regime of Hitler was domestically tranquil. Totalitarian regimes are imperialistic and expansionistic in orientation. The territorial expansion of the United States was mostly internal with peripheral expansion into the Pacific. The argument that the United States is an imperial power because it expanded from coast to coast does not prove that democracy and imperialism are exclusive of each other. Manifest Destiny, the movement westward, was a form of continental American expansion that happened in the nineteenth century, a century of imperialism and exploration. But what was acceptable in the nineteenth century is not acceptable in the twentieth, and the Cold War was not an imperialist design. Democratic systems are not necessarily noninterventionist. This is what their security requires. But democracies are not imperialistic in the sense of nineteenth-century atavistic, colonial imperialism. In fact, Wilsonianism is the expression of an American influence without imperialism. Searching for military bases in the Pacific was part and parcel of nineteenth-century American expansion in the name of security. It involved the United States in wars in the Philippines and the Caribbean.

Democracy has now been challenged by ethnicity in Great Britain by the Irish and Scots, in Belgium by the Walloons, in Spain by the Catalans and Basques, and in the Balkans and the Middle East. But as Britain, Belgium, and Spain demonstrate, democracy is not expansionist and can tolerate minority groups and ethnic groups better than any other system. Nevertheless, the Wilsonian ideals based on the American experience of federalism and states' rights are precisely what President Clinton believes. The hope of the Clinton administration is that the former Soviet Union will become a federal state in the Wilsonian tradition, without overtly touting Wilsonianism. Democracy is preferable, but not required, for any stable international system. Peace is not guaranteed by democratic systems, nor is aggression uniquely the property of totalitarians. There is no political or intellectual reason for the establishment of a new world order. A new world order must be unique, ideologically motivated, and supported by conflicting and rival hegemonial powers. World orders come and go. When one dies, there is no need to assume that the unimaginable variety of ways that nations deal with one another requires that another be cobbled together in the lifetime of anyone who remembers the last.

PREFACE

1. Foglesong, *America's Secret War*, 293.
2. Ibid., 296.
3. Ibid., 297.
4. Ibid., 298.
5. I totally reject the concept developed by liberal and progressive intellectual historians that Franco's Spain was a fascist state. It was a corporatist, conservative, traditional state. In fact, it was an antifascist and an anticommunist state: Franco fought viciously against the fascist movement Falanga in Spain. See Payne, *Falange*. See also Payne, *Franco Regime*.
6. The reason why fascism is not included in this analysis, despite its important role in twentieth-century national and international politics, is that the fascist ideology weakened the Italian regime because Mussolini's aspirations, founded on fascist theories, did not match Italy's military and industrial capability. Italy's fascism would not have won a war if it had not been for the aid of Hitler's Nazi Germany. Thus Mussolini's aspirations for world order threatened rather than enhanced Italy's security. They were no more than exercises in grandeur and in grandstanding.
7. The most prominent neorealist is Waltz, *A Theory of International Politics*. See two special issues of *Security Studies* 5, nos. 1 and 2 (1996), on neorealism.
8. Richard Pipes, Robert Conquest, R. C. Raack, Mikhail Heller, and Alexandr Nekrich.

INTRODUCTION

1. Iran, for instance, is threatened by revolutionary movement. In the Moslem world, nationalism has been replaced by Islamic fundamentalism, another guise for Arab, Muslim, and Iranian nationalism.

CHAPTER ONE

1. This is a rather inexact paraphrasing of Payne, *History of Fascism*, 78–79.
2. Rothschild, *East Central Europe*, 8.
3. Ibid., 11.

4. Ibid., 13.

5. Ibid., 14–15.

6. Ibid., 21.

7. Weber, *Action Française*, is the outstanding study of the movement.

8. I have selected the most significant works done on Nazism, the police state, and Hitler. See Laqueur, *Fascism*; Bracher, *German Dictatorship*; Bracher, Sauer, and Schultz, *Die Nationalsozialistische Machtergreifung*; Broszat, *Hitler State*; Browder, *Foundations of the Nazi Police State*; Burleigh and Wippermann, *Racial State*; Fest, *Hitler*; Kershaw, *Nazi Dictatorship*; Mosse, *Crisis of German Ideology*; and Perlmutter, *Modern Authoritarianism*.

Interpretations of fascism vary, and there is no one definitive school of thought. I refuse to accept the inclusion of Nazism in the fascist genus simply because the fundamental difference between fascism and Nazism is racism. Although there were several racists in fascist movements, as there were among right-wing radical nationalists, the purpose of Nazism, the raison d'être behind Hitler's war, was the destruction of Jewry and the formation of a racial utopia. Here I beg to differ with the outstanding scholar Stanley Payne, in his most recent work, *History of Fascism*. Payne's book, in the words of James A. Gregor, is an encyclopedia of fascism and a tour de force. With this I agree. For fascism, see De Felice, *Interpretations of Fascism*; Gregor, *Fascist Persuasion*.

9. Rothschild, *East Central Europe*, 10.

10. Ibid.; Lukacs, *Great Powers*; Seton-Watson, *Eastern Europe*; Macartney, *National States*; Rogger and Weber, *European Right*.

11. Mayer, *Political Origins of the New Diplomacy of Peace-Making*; Mayer, *Political Origins of the New Diplomacy*; Kettle, *The Allies and the Russian Collapse*.

12. Lukacs, *Great Powers*, quoting Hoffmann, 9.

13. See Chapter 3 for references on communism.

14. Feldman, *Great Disorder*; James, *German Slump*; Kent, *Spoils of War*.

15. Walt, *Revolution and War*, 127.

16. Ibid., 32.

17. Ibid., 33.

18. Ibid., 37.

CHAPTER TWO

1. The best analysis of Wilson's ideology is Levin, *Woodrow Wilson and World Politics*. The best recent analysis is Knock, *To End All Wars*. Other good works are Arthur Link's biographies of Wilson; Ambro-

sius, *Woodrow Wilson and the American Diplomatic Tradition*; and Nordholt, *Woodrow Wilson*.

2. Heater, *National Self-Determination*, 9.

3. Tucker and Hendrickson, *Empire of Liberty*, 231–38.

4. Levin, *Woodrow Wilson and World Politics*, 2–3.

5. Much has been written on the Paris Peace Conference and the Treaty of Versailles. Thomas Knock's outstanding analysis of the origin of the League is extremely instructive (*To End All Wars*, vii, 31–70).

6. Ibid., vii.

7. Ibid., 37.

8. Ibid., 55.

9. Examples are George Bush calling Saddam Hussein "Adolf Hitler," as well as the Cold War presidents conceiving Stalin as Attila the Hun and the Soviet system as an "evil empire."

10. Raack, *Stalin's Drive to the West*.

11. Schwabe, *Woodrow Wilson*, 402.

12. Ibid., 406–7.

13. Captain Alfred Mahan, the naval American realpolitiker, argued that to fulfill the role of sea power in history, the United States must dominate the ocean to extend American influence to the Pacific. Although international conflicts are not dependent upon sea power, sea power is critical. See Mahan, *The Influence of Sea Power upon History*.

14. Challener, *Admirals, Generals, and American Foreign Policy*, 12–45.

15. Ibid., 12.

16. Combs, *American Diplomatic History*, 74.

17. Collin, *Theodore Roosevelt*, 107–8.

18. Ibid., 118.

19. Cooper, *The Warrior and the Priest*, xi.

20. Ibid., xii.

21. Ibid.

22. Ibid., xiii.

23. Collin, "Symbolism versus Hegemony," 473. Also see Healy, *Drive to Hegemony*; Collin, *Theodore Roosevelt's Caribbean*.

24. Collin, "Symbolism versus Hegemony," 471.

25. Cooper states that "Hoover's politics, at home and abroad, represented at least a selective adaptation of Roosevelt's and Wilson's legacies" (*The Warrior and the Priest*, 347).

26. Johnson, *Peace Progressives*, 3.

27. Ibid.

28. Ibid., 75.

29. Taken from a speech by Senator Gronna, quoted ibid., 99.

30. Ibid., 100.

31. Ibid., 105.

32. Ibid., 150.

33. Combs, *American Diplomatic History*, 136.

34. Hunt, *Ideology and U.S. Foreign Policy*, 173.

35. Ibid., 183.

36. Ibid., 173.

37. Weinberg, *The Foreign Policy of Hitler's Germany*, 357.

38. Ibid., 360.

39. Welles, *Seven Decisions That Shaped History*, 177–78, quoted in Wilson, *First Summit*, 173. Also see Mayer, *Political Origins of the New Diplomacy of Peace-Making*, 229–83, for a left-wing historian's perspective.

40. Borkenau, *World Communism*.

CHAPTER THREE

1. McKenzie, *Comintern and World Revolution*, 4.

2. Levin, *Woodrow Wilson and World Politics*, 13.

3. Lenin, *Imperialism*.

4. Mayer, *Political Origins of the New Diplomacy*, 35.

5. Borkenau, *World Communism*, 33.

6. On the Spanish Civil War see Bolloten, *Spanish Revolution*. On the Stalinist Comintern's role see Richardson, *Comintern Army*. Also see Brenan, *Spanish Labyrinth*.

7. Richardson, *Comintern Army*, 90.

8. On the French party, see Carr, *Twilight of the Comintern*, 150–207; and Borkenau, *World Communism*, 115–62.

9. Koch, *Double Lives*, 3, 44.

10. Koestler, *Arrow in the Blue*.

11. The best account of Stalin's *Drang Nach Westen* can be found in Raack, *Stalin's Drive to the West*.

12. Ibid., 3–4.

13. Ibid., 9.

14. Ibid., 14.

15. Ibid., 16, 21.

16. Ibid., 21.

17. Ibid., 24.

18. Ibid., 32.

19. Ibid., 38.

20. Ibid., 69.

21. Ibid., 71.

22. Ibid., 102.

23. Ibid., 112.

24. Ibid., 114.

25. Ibid., 119.

26. Ibid., 165.

27. For a detailed and analytical study of Stalin and his ally FDR, see Perlmutter, *FDR and Stalin*.

28. Raack, *Stalin's Drive to the West*, 146.

29. Ibid., 128.

30. Ibid., 135.

31. Ibid.

32. Ibid., 150.

33. Ibid., 151.

34. Ibid.

CHAPTER FOUR

1. On Hitler's racial state, see Burleigh and Wippermann, *Racial State*, 23–28. Also see Kershaw, *Nazi Dictatorship*.

2. Hamerow, *On the Road to the Wolf's Lair*, 65.

3. An outstanding study is Weindling, *Health, Race and German Politics*.

4. Ibid., 25.

5. Ibid., 28.

6. Ibid., 36–38.

7. Ibid., 48.

8. Burleigh and Wippermann, *Racial State*, 30.

9. Ibid., 35.

10. Ibid., 63.

11. Ibid., 70.

12. Ibid., 38.

13. Ibid., 490.

14. Rich, *Hitler's War Aims*, xi.

15. Ibid.

16. Ibid., xii.

17. Ibid., xiii.

18. The most extensive analyses of the SS are Krausnick et al., *Anatomy of the SS State*; and Wegner, *Waffen SS*. See also Koehl, *Black Corps*; and Kershaw, *Nazi Dictatorship*.

19. Krausnick et al., *Anatomy of the SS State*, 40.

20. Ibid., 43.

21. Burleigh, *Germany Turns Eastward*, 8; see also 162, 163, 216, 217.

22. Krausnick et al., *Anatomy of the SS State*, 510–11.

23. Burleigh, *Germany Turns Eastward*, 510–12.

24. Ibid., 167.

25. Ibid., 166–67.

26. Ibid.

27. Wegner, *Waffen SS*, 11.

28. See Carr, *Twenty Years Crisis*; Azema, *From Munich to the Liberation of France*; Berghahn, *Modern Germany*; Ulam, *Stalin*.

CHAPTER FIVE

1. Kimball, *Churchill and Roosevelt*, 1:227–28.

2. The best book on the Atlantic Charter is Wilson, *First Summit*, 173–202.

3. Ibid., 173.

4. Ibid., 174.

5. Churchill, paraphrased ibid., 88.

6. This idea was based on not very substantial statements by Roosevelt and reports by the Department of State, which certainly did not see eye to eye with the president.

7. Aga-Rossi, "Roosevelt's European Policy and the Origins of the Cold War," 73–74.

8. Kimball, unpublished paper, presented at Naval Conference at Contigny, April 1994.

9. Gardner, *Spheres of Influence*, xii.

10. Ibid., xiii.

11. Kimball, *The Juggler*, 97.

12. Ibid.

13. Ibid.

14. Kimball, unpublished paper, 3.

15. Aga-Rossi, "Roosevelt's European Policy and the Origins of the Cold War," 73.

16. Examples are the October 5, 1937, Quarantine the Aggressors speech (a speech without teeth) and the few pieces he wrote on Latin America. The speech may be found in *Foreign Relations of the United States, 1937,* 1:665–70.

17. Aga-Rossi, "Roosevelt's European Policy and the Origins of the Cold War," 65–85.

18. Perlmutter, *FDR and Stalin*.

19. Kimball, unpublished paper, 4.

20. Perlmutter, *FDR and Stalin*.

21. Kennan and Lukacs, "From World War," 49–50.

22. Ibid., 52.

23. Ibid.

24. Ibid.

25. Ibid.

26. Ibid., 59.

CHAPTER SIX

1. Kennan, *American Diplomacy*; Kennan, *Memoirs*; [Kennan] "X," "The Sources of Soviet Conduct," 566–82; Hixson, *George F. Kennan*; Miscamble, *George F. Kennan and the Making of American Foreign Policy*; Mayers, *George Kennan and the Dilemmas of U.S. Foreign Policy*; Gaddis, *Strategies of Containment*; Isaacson and Thomas, *Wise Men*; Gaddis, *The United States and the End of the Cold War*; Smith, *Realist Thought from Weber to Kissinger*, especially the section on Kennan, 165–91; de Santis, *Diplomacy of Silence*.

2. "George F. Kennan and George Urban: A Conversation," in *Encounters with Kennan*, 1–84.

3. Kennan and Lukacs, "From World War," 51–52.

4. Gaddis, *Strategies of Containment*, 27.

5. Hogan, *Marshall Plan*, 4.

6. Miscamble, *George F. Kennan and the Making of American Foreign Policy*.

7. Hogan, *Marshall Plan*, 26–27.

8. Combs, "The Compromise That Never Was," 366.

9. Ibid.

10. Ibid., 367.

11. Ibid., 365.

12. Ibid., 366.

13. Gaddis and Nitze, "NSC 68 and the Soviet Threat Reconsidered," 5.

14. Ibid., 6.

15. Some of these ideas are taken from Combs, "The Compromise That Never Was."

16. Gaddis and Nitze, "NSC 68 and the Soviet Threat Reconsidered," 2.

17. Ibid., 3.

18. Ibid., 4.

19. Alonzo Hamby has, in my view, a most persuasive argument regarding Truman and the bomb: *The Life of Harry S. Truman*, 331–45, 444–45, 524–25. For those who believe the bomb should not have been used, see the torrent of articles by Barton Bernstein and the new work by Gar Alperovitz, *The Decision to Use the Atomic Bomb*.

20. Wohlstetter, "The Delicate Balance of Terror," 65.

21. Larson, *Origins of Containment*.

22. Hogan, *Marshall Plan*, 6.

23. Ninkovich, *Modernity and Power*, 37.
24. Taken from President Clinton's televised address to the nation on November 28, 1995, quoted in the *New York Times*, November 28, 1995, A14.
25. Mills, *Power Elite*.
26. Yergin, *Shattered Peace*.

CHAPTER SEVEN

1. Mastny, *Cold War and Soviet Insecurity*, 191.
2. Zubok and Pleshakov, *Inside the Kremlin's Cold War*.
3. Holloway, *Stalin and the Bomb*.
4. Zubok and Pleshakov, *Inside the Kremlin's Cold War*.
5. Ibid., 174.
6. Ibid., 182.
7. Ibid., 184.
8. Ibid., 195.
9. Ibid., 203.
10. Perlmutter, *FDR and Stalin*.
11. Zubok and Pleshakov, *Inside the Kremlin's Cold War*, 239.

CHAPTER EIGHT

1. Brody et al., *Absolute Weapon*.
2. Heilbrun, "Revision Thing," 33.
3. Wright, *Study of International Relations*.
4. Morgenthau, *Politics among Nations*, 4–15.

Aga-Rossi, Elena. "Roosevelt's European Policy and the Origins of the Cold War: A Reevaluation." *Telos* 96 (Summer 1993): 65–85.

Alperovitz, Gar. *The Decision to Use the Bomb and the Architecture of an American Myth*. New York: Knopf, 1995.

Ambrosius, Lloyd E. *Woodrow Wilson and the American Diplomatic Tradition: The Treaty Fight in Perspective*. New York: Cambridge University Press, 1987.

Azema, Jean-Pierre. *From Munich to the Liberation of France, 1938–1944*. Paris: Seuil, 1979.

Berghahn, V. R. *Modern Germany: Society, Economy and Politics in the Twentieth Century*. Cambridge: Cambridge University Press, 1982.

Bernstein, Benton. "The Atomic Bomb and American Foreign Policy, 1941–1945." *Peace and Change* 2 (Spring 1974): 1–6.

———. "Writing, Righting, or Wrongdoing the Historical Record: President Truman's Letter on His Atomic Bomb Decision." *Diplomatic History* 16 (Winter 1992): 163–73.

Bolloten, Burnett. *The Spanish Civil War: Revolution and Counter-Revolution*. Chapel Hill: University of North Carolina Press, 1991.

Borkenau, Franz. *World Communism*. New York: Norton, 1939.

Bracher, Karl D. *German Dictatorship: The Origins, Structure, and Effects of National Socialism*. Translated from the German by Jean Steinberg. Introduction by Peter Gay. New York: Praeger, 1970.

Bracher, Karl D., W. Sauer, and G. Schultz. *Die Nationalsozialistische Machtergreifung: Studien zur Errichtung des Totalitaren Herrschaftssystems in Deutschland 1933/34*. 2 durchgesehene Aufl. Cologne: Westdeutscher Verlag, 1962.

Brenan, Gerald. *The Spanish Labyrinth: An Account of the Social and Political Background of the Civil War*. 2d ed. Cambridge: Cambridge University Press, 1950.

Brody, Richard, et al. *The Absolute Weapon: Atomic Power and World Order*. New York: Harcourt, Brace, 1946.

Broszat, Martin. *The Hitler State: The Foundation and Development of the Internal Structure of the Third Reich*. Translated by John W. Hiden. New York: Longman, 1981.

Browder, G. C. *Foundations of the Nazi Police State: The Formation of Sipo and SC*. Lexington: University Press of Kentucky, 1990.

Burleigh, Michael. *Germany Turns Eastward*. Cambridge: Cambridge University Press, 1988.

Burleigh, Michael, and Wolfgang Wippermann. *The Racial State: Germany, 1933–1945*. Cambridge: Cambridge University Press, 1991.

Carr, E. H. *Twenty Years Crisis, 1919–1939: An Introduction to the Study of International Relations*. 2d ed. New York: St. Martin's Press, 1956.

———. *The Twilight of the Comintern, 1930–1935*. New York: Pantheon Books, 1982.

Challener, Richard D. *Admirals, Generals, and American Foreign Policy, 1898–1914*. Princeton: Princeton University Press, 1973.

Clinton, William. A televised address to the nation on November 28, 1995, quoted in the *New York Times*, November 28, 1995, A14.

Collin, Richard H. "Symbolism versus Hegemony: New Directions in the Foreign Relations Historiography of Theodore Roosevelt and William Howard Taft." *Diplomatic History* 19 (Summer 1995): 473–97.

———. *Theodore Roosevelt, Culture, Diplomacy, and Expansion: A New View of American Imperialism*. Baton Rouge: Louisiana State University Press, 1985.

———. *Theodore Roosevelt's Caribbean: The Panama Canal, the Monroe Doctrine, and the Latin American Context*. Baton Rouge: Louisiana State University Press, 1990.

Combs, Jerald A. *American Diplomatic History: Two Centuries of Changing Interpretations*. Berkeley: University of California Berkeley, 1983.

———. "The Compromise That Never Was: George Kennan, Paul Nitze, and the Issue of Conventional Deterrence in Europe, 1949–1952." *Diplomatic History* 15 (Summer 1991): 361–86.

Conquest, Robert. *The Great Terror: A Reassessment*. New York: Oxford University Press, 1990.

Cooper, John Milton, Jr. *The Warrior and the Priest: Woodrow Wilson and Theodore Roosevelt*. Cambridge, Mass.: Belknap Press of Harvard University Press, 1983.

De Felice, Renzo. *Interpretations of Fascism*. Translated by Brenda Huff Everett. Cambridge, Mass.: Harvard University Press, 1977.

de Santis, Hugh. *The Diplomacy of Silence: The American Foreign Service, the Soviet Union and the Cold War, 1933–1947*. Chicago: University of Chicago Press, 1980.

Feldman, Gerald D. *The Great Disorder: Politics, Economics and Society in German Inflation, 1914–1924*. New York: Oxford University Press, 1993.

Fest, Joachim. *Hitler*. Translated from the German by Richard and Clara Winston. New York: Harcourt Brace Jovanovich, 1974.

Foglesong, David. *America's Secret War against Bolshevism: U.S. Intervention in the Russian Civil War, 1917–1920*. Chapel Hill: University of North Carolina Press, 1995.

Gaddis, John L. *Strategies of Containment: A Critical Reappraisal of Post-War American National Security Policy*. New York: Oxford University Press, 1992.

——. *The United States and the End of the Cold War: Implications, Reconsiderations, Provocations*. New York: Oxford University Press, 1992.

Gaddis, John L., and Paul Nitze. "NSC 68 and the Soviet Threat Reconsidered." *International Security* (Spring 1980).

Gardner, Lloyd. *Spheres of Influence: The Great Powers Partition Europe, from Munich to Yalta*. Chicago: Ivan Dee, 1993.

"George F. Kennan and George Urban: A Conversation." In *Encounters with Kennan: The Great Debate*, 1–84. London: Frank Cass, 1979.

Gregor, James A. *The Fascist Persuasion in Radical Politics*. Princeton: Princeton University Press, 1974.

Hamby, Alonzo. *The Life of Harry S. Truman: Man of the People*. New York: Oxford University Press, 1995.

Hamerow, Theodore S. *On the Road to the Wolf's Lair: German Resistance to Hitler*. Cambridge, Mass.: Harvard University Press, 1997.

Healy, David. *Drive to Hegemony: The United States in the Caribbean, 1898–1917*. Madison: University of Wisconsin Press, 1988.

Heater, Derek. *National Self-Determination: Woodrow Wilson and His Legacy*. New York: St. Martin's Press, 1994.

Heilbrun, Jacob. "The Revision Thing." *New Republic* 211 (April 15, 1994): 31–39.

Heller, Mikhail, and Alexandr Nekrich. *The History of the Soviet Union from 1917 to the Present*. Translated fron the Russian by Phyllis Carlos. New York: Summit Books, 1986.

Hixson, Walter L. *George F. Kennan: Cold War Iconoclast*. New York: Columbia University Press, 1989.

Hobson, John. *Imperialism*. London: G. Allen & Unwin, 1938.

Hogan, Michael. *The Marshall Plan: Americans, British, and the Reconstruction of Western Europe, 1949–1952*. Cambridge: Cambridge University Press, 1989.

Holborn, Hajo. *A History of Modern Germany*. New York: Knopf, 1959.

——. *Republic to Reich: The Making of the Nazi Revolution, Ten Essays*. Translated from the German by Ralph Manheim. New York: Pantheon Books, 1972.

Holloway, David. *Stalin and the Bomb: The Soviet Union and Atomic Energy, 1939–1956*. New Haven: Yale University Press, 1994.

Hunt, Michael H. *Ideology and U.S. Foreign Policy*. New Haven: Yale University Press, 1987.

Isaacson, Walter, and Evan Thomas. *The Wise Men: Six Friends and the World They Made, Acheson, Bohlen, Harriman, Kennan, Lovett, McCloy*. New York: Simon & Schuster, 1986.

James, Harold. *The German Slump: Politics and Economics, 1924–1926*. New York: Oxford University Press, 1986.

Johnson, Robert David. *The Peace Progressives and American Foreign Relations*. Cambridge, Mass.: Harvard University Press, 1995.

Kennan, George F. *American Diplomacy, 1900–1950*. Rev. ed. New York: Oxford University Press, 1991.

———. *Memoirs, 1925–1950*. Boston: Little, Brown, 1967.

[Kennan, George F.] "X." "The Sources of Soviet Conduct." *Foreign Affairs* 25 (July 1947): 566–82.

Kennan, George F., and John Lukacs. "From World War to Cold War (an exchange of letters)." *American Heritage* 46 (December 1995): 42–67.

Kent, Bruce. *The Spoils of War: The Politics, Economics and Diplomacy of Reparations, 1918–1932*. New York: Oxford University Press, 1989.

Kershaw, Ian. *The Nazi Dictatorship: Problems and Perspectives of Interpretation*. London: Edward Arnold, 1985.

Kettle, Michael. *The Allies and the Russian Collapse, March 1917 to March 1918*. Vol 1. Minneapolis: University of Minnesota Press, 1981.

Kimball, Warren. *Churchill and Roosevelt: The Complete Correspondence*. Princeton: Princeton University Press, 1984.

———. *The Juggler: Franklin Roosevelt as Wartime Statesman*. Princeton: Princeton University Press, 1991.

———. Unpublished paper presented at Naval Conference at Contigny, April 1994.

Knock, Thomas J. *To End All Wars: Woodrow Wilson and the Quest for a New World Order*. New York: Oxford University Press, 1992.

Koch, Stephen. *Double Lives: Spies and Writers in the Secret Soviet War of Ideas against the West*. New York: Maxwell Macmillan International, 1994.

Koehl, Robert. *The Black Corps: The Structure and Power Struggles of the Nazi S.S.* Madison: University of Wisconsin Press, 1983.

Koestler, Arthur. *Arrow in the Blue*. New York: Macmillan, 1970.

Krausnick, Helmut, et al., eds. *Anatomy of the SS State*. New York: Walker, 1968.

Langer, William. *The Diplomacy of Imperialism*. 2d ed. New York: Knopf, 1968.

Laqueur, Walter, ed. *Fascism: A Reader's Guide, Analyses, Interpretations, Bibliography*. Berkeley: University of California Press, 1976.

Larson, Deborah Welch. *Origins of Containment: A Psychological Explanation*. Princeton: Princeton University Press, 1985.

Lenin, V. I. *Imperialism: The Highest Stage of Capitalism*. New York: International Publishers, 1939.

Levin, N. Gordon, Jr. *Wilson*. Princeton: Princeton University Press, 1947.

———. *Wilson the Diplomatist: A Look at His Major Foreign Policies*. Baltimore: Johns Hopkins Press, 1957.

———. *Woodrow Wilson and World Politics*. New York: Oxford University Press, 1968.

Link, Arthur. *Woodrow Wilson and the Progressive Era, 1910–1917*. New York: Harper & Row, 1953.

Lukacs, John A. *The Great Powers and Eastern Europe*. New York: American Book Company, 1953.

Macartney, C. A. *National States and National Minorities*. New York: Russell and Russell, 1968.

McKenzie, Kermit. *Comintern and World Revolution, 1928–1947: The Shaping of Doctrine*. New York: Columbia University Press, 1964.

Mahan, Alfred. *The Influence of Sea Power upon History, 1660–1783*. London: Sampson, Law, Martson, 1890.

Mastny, Vojtech. *The Cold War Soviet Insecurity: The Stalin Years*. New York: Oxford University Press, 1996.

Mayer, Arno J. *Political Origins of the New Diplomacy, 1917–1918*. New Haven: Yale University Press, 1959.

———. *Political Origins of the New Diplomacy of Peace-Making: Containment and Counterrevolution at Versailles, 1918–1919*. New York: Knopf, 1967.

Mayers, David Allen. *George Kennan and the Dilemmas of U.S. Foreign Policy*. New York: Oxford University Press, 1988.

Mills, C. Wright. *The Power Elite*. New York: Oxford University Press, 1956.

Miscamble, Wilson D. *George F. Kennan and the Making of American Foreign Policy, 1947–1950*. Princeton: Princeton University Press, 1992.

Morgenthau, Hans. *Politics among Nations: The Struggle for Power and Peace*. New York: Knopf, 1973.

Mosse, George. *The Crisis of German Ideology: Intellectual Origins of the Third Reich*. New York: Grosset and Dunlap, 1964.

Ninkovich, Frank. *Modernity and Power: A History of the Domino Theory in the Twentieth Century*. Chicago: University of Chicago Press, 1994.

Nordholt, Jan Willem. *Woodrow Wilson: A Life for World Peace*. Berkeley: University of California Press, 1991.

Payne, Stanley. *Falange: A History of Spanish Fascism*. 2d ed. Stanford: Stanford University Press, 1979.

———. *The Franco Regime, 1936–1975*. Madison: University of Wisconsin Press, 1987.

———. *A History of Fascism, 1914–1945*. Madison: University of Wisconsin Press, 1995.

Perlmutter, Amos. *FDR and Stalin: A Not-So Grand Alliance*. Columbia: University of Missouri Press, 1993.

———. *Modern Authoritarianism: A Comparative Institutional Analysis*. New Haven: Yale University Press, 1981.

Pipes, Richard. *A Concise History of the Russian Revolution*. New York: Knopf, 1995.

Puleston, W. D. *Mahan: The Life and Work of Captain Alfred Thayer Mahan*. New Haven: Yale University Press, 1939.

Raack, R. C. *Stalin's Drive to the West, 1938–1945: The Origins of the Cold War*. Stanford: Stanford University Press, 1995.

Rich, Norman. *Hitler's War Aims: The Establishment of a New Order*. New York: Norton, 1973.

Richardson, R. Dan. *Comintern Army: The International Brigades and the Spanish Civil War*. Lexington: University Press of Kentucky, 1982.

Rogger, Hans, and Eugen Weber, eds. *The European Right: A Historical Profile*. Berkeley: University of California Press, 1965.

Rothschild, Joseph. *East Central Europe between the Two World Wars*. Seattle: University of Washington Press, 1974.

Schwabe, Klaus. *Woodrow Wilson, Revolutionary Germany, and Peacemaking, 1918–1919: Missionary Diplomacy and the Realities of Power*. Chapel Hill: University of North Carolina Press, 1985.

Seton-Watson, Hugh. *Eastern Europe between the Wars, 1918–1941*. 3d ed. Hamden, Conn.: Archon Books, 1962.

Smith, Michael Joseph. *Realist Thought from Weber to Kissinger*. Baton Rouge: Louisiana State University Press, 1986.

Tansill, Charles. *America Goes to War*. Boston: Little, Brown, 1938.

Taylor, A. J. P. *The Origins of the Second World War*. London: Hamish Hamilton, 1961.

Tucker, Robert W., and David Hendrickson. *Empire of Liberty: The Statecraft of Thomas Jefferson*. New York: Oxford University Press, 1990.

Ulam, Adam. *Stalin: The Man and His Era*. New York: Viking Press, 1973.

Walker, Martin. *The Cold War: A History*. New York: Henry Holt, 1994.

Walt, Steven. *Revolution and War*. Ithaca: Cornell University Press, 1996.

Waltz, Kenneth. *Man, the State, and War: A Theoretical Analysis*. New York: Columbia University Press, 1959.

———. *A Theory of International Politics*. New York: Random House, 1979.

Weber, Eugen. *Action Française: Royalism and Reaction in Twentieth-Century France*. Stanford: Stanford University Press, 1962.

Wegner, Brend. *The Waffen SS: Organization, Ideology, and Function*. London: Basil Blackwell, 1990.

Weinberg, Gerhard. *The Foreign Policy of Hitler's Germany: Diplomatic Revolution in Europe, 1933–1938*. Chicago: University of Chicago Press, 1970.

Weindling, Paul. *Health, Race and German Politics between National Unification and Nazism, 1870–1945*. New York: Cambridge University Press, 1989.

Welles, Sumner. *Seven Decisions That Shaped History*. New York: Harper, 1951.

Whealey, Robert. *Hitler and Spain: The Nazi Role in the Spanish Civil War, 1936–1939*. Lexington: University Press of Kentucky, 1989.

Wilson, Theodore. *The First Summit: Roosevelt and Churchill at Placentia Bay, 1941*. Boston: Houghton Mifflin, 1969.

Wohlstetter, Albert. "The Delicate Balance of Terror." *Foreign Affairs* 37 (January 1959).

Wright, Quincy. *The Study of International Relations*. New York: Appleton-Century-Crofts, 1955.

Yergin, Daniel. *Shattered Peace: The Origins of the Cold War and the National Security State*. Boston: Houghton Mifflin, 1977.

Zubok, Vladislav, and Constantin Pleshakov. *Inside the Kremlin's Cold War: From Stalin to Khrushchev*. Cambridge, Mass.: Harvard University Press, 1996.

and atomic bombing of Japan, 130
Truman administration, 122
Tucker, Robert W., 36
Turkey, 130, 162–63, 165
Turner, Frederick Jackson, 42

Ukraine, 94, 165
Ulbricht, Walter, 77
Union for Democratic Control (UDC), 33
United Nations, 7, 13; Roosevelt and, 37, 99, 102, 103, 105, 106, 129, 133, 136; United States and, 41, 105, 133; nationalism and, 53; and collective security, 99, 102, 105–6, 111, 135–36; Stalin and, 101, 102, 103, 105, 106, 129; Security Council, 105, 136; Cold War and, 106; founding of, 129, 137; Third World and, 134; nuclear weapons and, 156
Urban, George, 120

Versailles Treaty (1919), 12; France and, 16–17, 95; and European instability, 19–21, 55, 56; Hitler and, 21, 25; Wilson and, 27, 38–40, 58, 137
Vietnam War, 49, 50, 51, 52
Virchow, Rudolph, 84

Waffen SS, 91, 93
Warsaw Pact, 131, 133
Webb, James, 157
Weinberg, Gerhard, 57
Wells, H. G., 72–73
West Germany, 146
Wharton, Edith, 28
White, Andrew D., 42
Wilson, Theodore, 99
Wilson, Woodrow: and covert action, ix, x, 32, 34, 113, 151;

and internationalism, x, 29, 32–33, 34–35, 43–44, 46, 47–48, 65, 137; and League of Nations, x, 32, 35–36, 81, 137, 138; and Russian civil war, x, 36; and Cold War, x, 155; and new world order, 5, 6, 10, 12–13, 30–31, 81, 88, 94, 96–97, 117, 135, 140; and U.S. foreign policy, 5, 6, 28, 30, 33–34, 40–41, 45, 106, 120, 137–38; and American exceptionalism, 5, 30–31, 32; and democracy, 19, 32, 35, 87, 159, 165, 166; and Versailles Treaty, 27, 38–40, 58, 137; influence on presidency, 28, 45; background, 28–30; FDR and, 29; and imperialism, 29, 31–32, 44–45, 61, 65; and Theodore Roosevelt, 29, 43–45; and free trade, 29, 64; and national self-determination, 30, 52–53, 66; and World War I, 31–32, 63, 115–16, 154–55; and Lenin, 32, 60, 61, 62–63, 64, 159; in election of 1912, 34; and collective security, 34, 35, 47, 66–67; and balance of power, 34, 46; and Fourteen Points, 38, 39, 47, 58; and ideology, 83; Kennan and, 120
Wilsonian world order: and U.S. intervention, ix, 41, 137, 166; neo-Wilsonianism, xiii, 130, 161–62; persistence of, 3, 14–15, 53–54; and U.S. foreign policy, 5, 6, 36, 38, 40–41, 134, 137, 161, 165; Leninist and Nazi orders versus, 5, 6, 66, 95, 117; Clinton and, 5, 15, 37–38, 45, 53–54, 139, 166; isolationists and, 47–48; nationalism and, 56, 66; and Cold War, 66,